Praise for *Uncontrived Mindfulness: Ending Suffering through Attention, Curiosity and Wisdom*

Vajradevi is a practitioner who shares her own experience of practising mindfulness simply and clearly. She makes traditional concepts accessible because she knows them from the inside, and *Uncontrived Mindfulness* is full of stories of how Vajradevi has learned to be mindful of her own life. The uncontrived relaxation of her writing matches her message that mindfulness isn't a technique or an achievement so much as a 'wise involvement with experiences' that is both focused and at ease. – **Vishvapani Blomfield**, author of *Gautama Buddha: The Life and Teachings of the Awakened One*

A wonderful book, written with that independence of mind characteristic of deep practitioners. Reading is like being taken into the author's mind: just the tone reveals how what's being described is affecting her. – **Kamalashila**, meditation teacher and author of *Buddhist Meditation: Tranquillity, Imagination & Insight*

Vajradevi gives relevant and real examples which show us that dedicating ourselves to mindfulness does not mean being cut off from life. I loved reading the stories she weaves in to explain her journey in mindfulness and the thoughtful connections she makes with common doubts or questions about the practice, the journey, and its effects – a true friend to everyone who is practising or wishes to approach the practice.

Uncontrived Mindfulness really helps to demystify meditation and mindfulness in a thorough, relevant way that is light and even humorous! Vajradevi demonstrates through every page that mindfulness can be in every or any moment, hence uncontrived. Just open to any chapter or page and find the fascinating ways that our ordinary or thoughtful moments can all be part of mindfulness practice. – **Ma Thet**, translator for Sayadaw U Tejaniya

Vajradevi's approach to satipaṭṭhāna – mindfulness and meditation – is both refreshing and distinct. There are already many excellent books that go into the details of the *Satipaṭṭhāna Sutta* and the technicalities of the original Pali terminology, and a vast plethora of general books about mindfulness. Vajradevi takes us straight into the experiential core to which these teachings are pointing. This is mindfulness as the direct way to awakening from the delusions which produce our suffering. 'McMindfulness' it is definitely not! Her own substantial practice, together with the benefits of having studied satipaṭṭhāna with some very good teachers, shines through.

It makes a huge difference to realize that effective mindfulness practice does not have to be constantly effortful and contrived. Vajradevi points us to the awareness that is already naturally present – hence, 'uncontrived mindfulness'. As I've found out myself, recognizing this does make all the difference to practice. The simple, lucid style, personal stories, and practical exercises make this into an extraordinarily hands-on and helpful book for new and experienced meditators alike. – **Tejananda John Wakeman**, Chair, Vajraloka Meditation Retreat Centre, North Wales

This is a lively and accessible overview of the transformative power of mindful awareness in the cultivation of a free and awakened life. It is clearly a distillation of many years of dedicated practice, and the writing is enlivened by personal glimpses into the author's own journey as well as reflective exercises to help the reader directly connect with what is being described. If you've ever felt that your mindfulness practice was becoming somewhat 'contrived' – trying too hard, or over-striving for results – the guidance in these pages will support you in undoing that. Vajradevi's writing is based on a deep understanding of the mind and how its habits can lead us into suffering or toward release. – **Jenny Wilks**, Insight Meditation teacher, Gaia House Retreat Centre, Devon

Uncontrived Mindfulness is a treasure for anyone interested in living a mindful and wise life. Vajradevi has the ability to *translate* the Buddha's classical teachings on mindfulness and wisdom into clear and practical instructions for both formal meditation and daily life. She offers her guidance, which is clearly based in her own deep and long experience, with such accessible examples and good humour that one finds it easy to trust and follow them . . . and come to recognize for oneself that uncontrived mindfulness is natural and universal. Many of her descriptions of uncontrived mindfulness, and the wisdom and freedom that naturally arise with it, are drawn from her own experiences in meditation and in daily life. The result, for me, was a deepening of the realization that mindfulness and wisdom are about how we live, and that this is supported by our formal meditation practice.

I can recommend this book both for those in the early days of learning to recognize and support uncontrived mindfulness, as well as for anyone who would like to refresh their approach to practice. Vajradevi reminds us of the joy that arises naturally as we relax into steady mindfulness and allow ourselves to recognize the wisdom of the Buddha. – **Carol Wilson**, Guiding Teacher of Insight Meditation Society

Uncontrived Mindfulness

Ending Suffering through Attention, Curiosity and Wisdom

Vajradevi

(*w*) indhorse Publications

Windhorse Publications
38 Newmarket Road
Cambridge
CB5 8DT
info@windhorsepublications.com
windhorsepublications.com

Cover design by Katarzyna Manecka

Typesetting and layout Tarajyoti
Printed by Bell & Bain Ltd, Glasgow

British Library Cataloguing in Publication Data:

A catalogue record for this book is available from the British Library.

ISBN: 978-1-911407-61-4

Contents

About the Author

Vajradevi (Karen Lambert) first met the Dharma in 1982 in Thailand at the age of twenty-two, and a year later connected with the Triratna community in London. She was ordained into the Triratna Buddhist Order in 1995 and worked in various Buddhist 'right livelihood' businesses, including helping establish Akashavana, a women's ordination retreat centre in Spain.

Vajradevi has been practising and teaching mindfulness with a strong insight dimension for over twenty-five years. To further her practice, she has studied with specialists in this approach, including Sayadaw U Pandita, Joseph Goldstein, and Bhikkhu Anālayo. She has spent a total of twelve months in Myanmar, on retreat with Sayadaw U Tejaniya.

Vajradevi leads retreats throughout the UK and Europe and her teaching is characterized by a deep love of and confidence in mindfulness as a path to wisdom. She emphasizes a receptive yet precise way of being aware that can be brought to any moment of our lives.

Vajradevi lives with her partner in Shropshire, England, where she is a Trustee and teacher at the Shrewsbury Buddhist Centre. You can read her meditation blog at www.uncontrivedmindfulness.net

Audio Downloads

This book has been produced with accompanying led meditations by the author, available as free downloads – see titles of meditations below. They can be streamed directly from the Web or downloaded in MP3 format. Please go to https://www.windhorsepublications. com/audio-resources/ and uncontrivedmindfulness.net

Chapter 1 – Led Meditation: Settling into Awareness
Chapter 2 – Led Meditation: Qualities of Awareness
Chapter 3 – Led Meditation: Knowing the Objects of Awareness
Chapter 4 – Led Meditation: Meditating with Right View
Chapter 5 – Led Meditation: Awareness of Difficult Mind States
Chapter 6 – Led Meditation: Meditating with Thinking
Chapter 7 – Led Meditation: Putting the Practice Together
Chapter 8 – Led Meditation: Aware of Awareness

Acknowledgements

My thanks and gratitude, first and foremost, to Bhante Sangharakshita and Sayadaw U Tejaniya who have both changed my life through their practice, teaching, and exemplification of the Dharma. It goes without saying that I would not have written this book without what I've learned from you both. Integrating my learnings from these two great teachers has been the work of many years' practice, and any errors contained in this presentation are of my own making.

My gratitude abounds to Jnanasiddhi for patiently helping to clarify my thinking and guiding me through the writing process, as well as editing the manuscript into a much-improved book. I feel you've been teaching me how to be a better writer. To be able to work closely with such a good friend on this project has been a delight.

My appreciation too, to Sagaraghosha who offered immensely helpful feedback on the first draft and encouraged me to keep going. And many thanks to Vajrapriya who was always willing to drop what he was doing, on the other side of our office, to read the latest version, and offer insightful and incisive comments.

Many thanks to the team at Windhorse Publications who have made the process far less intimidating than it otherwise would have been. They have been consistently friendly, flexible, helpful, and professional. I'm grateful to Priyananda, Dhammamegha, Helen, Michelle, Lee, and Caroline.

And finally, thank you to all the retreat centres that offer me the chance to communicate the Dharma through leading retreats, and to retreatants who come with their enthusiasm, integrity, and desire to practise. Having the opportunity to articulate one's understanding of the Dharma is a precious gift.

Publisher's Acknowledgements

Windhorse Publications wishes to gratefully acknowledge a grant from the Future Dharma Fund and Triratna European Chairs' Assembly Fund the towards the production of this book.

We also wish to acknowledge and thank the individual donors who gave to the book's production via our 'Sponsor-a-book' campaign.

Foreword

by Vidyamala

Vajradevi has given us a beautiful hymn to mindfulness and awareness as doorways to wisdom and freedom.

When reading her approach, it is immediately apparent that the *Satipaṭṭhāna Sutta*, one of the Buddha's seminal texts on mindfulness, has been her 'bible' for decades. Through her ongoing enquiry she has written a book that is a gift to us all. She communicates great knowledge of different aspects of the *sutta* with all their subtle nuances, whilst writing in a style that is very accessible and encouraging for everyone, whether you are a seasoned practitioner or a beginner.

I've known Vajradevi for many years and over this period I have seen her single-mindedly dedicate her life to plumbing the depths of what it means to live with a human mind. She has sat many long retreats, both in the UK and Myanmar, and shown great tenacity in her practice. The fruits of these many months of whole-hearted investigation of her inner world shine out from these pages.

She is also a woman with a great sense of adventure, and she writes in a style where diving into the heart/mind – the greatest possible adventure any of us can undertake – seems appealing and possible for anyone. I have an abiding memory of being on retreat with her back in the 1980s and coming into our shared dorm to find her dressed in a skydiving jumpsuit (because she found it comfy), doing a headstand against a wall. It was such a striking sight – quirky, hilarious – and I knew immediately that she was brave and liked to 'take the plunge' – quite literally when it came to skydiving! This same spirit of bravery and bold curiosity permeates these pages as she invites us to walk beside her while she quietly and skilfully unravels the many and varied ways we tie ourselves in mental and emotional knots of our own making. She is also generous in sharing personal anecdotes throughout the book, which brings the teachings to life in immediately accessible ways. It is lovely to drop into her world and get to know her as a flesh-and-blood human, working with, and learning from, her tendencies – tendencies many of us will recognize.

At the heart of the book is a radically simple approach to practice where the 'holy grail' is awareness itself, as a gateway to wisdom. Rather than worrying about 'what' you are experiencing, which can lead to lots of striving and blind alleys, the emphasis is on the quality of awareness and 'knowing' that we bring to whatever is showing up in all the moments that make up our lives. This leads to a relaxed, receptive approach to practice where any experience at all can be an opportunity for curiosity and freedom. Vajradevi repeatedly invites us to make less rather than more effort in how we approach the mind, a message that is gloriously simple and yet profoundly transformative.

She is also highly articulate about Right View and wisdom being the higher purpose and compass around which our mindfulness practice is oriented. Awareness is always practised in the service of freedom and the ending of suffering. As she says herself:

> What comes to mind is a simple phrase – awareness is transformative. I have a lot of faith and confidence that awareness can illuminate any aspect of my experience, that whatever I'm experiencing can be known in a way that allows it to be stripped of clinging, and therefore of suffering.

It is never easy to write a book, let alone to write a book where a profound understanding of complex and highly subtle teachings has been understood, digested, and then offered back to us in simple, approachable language imbued with clear common sense. Vajradevi has pulled off this feat.

In these pages, the Dharma comes across as compelling and inviting for anyone wanting to experience a wiser, kinder life.

Vidyamala Burch, co-founder of Breathworks, author of *Living Well with Pain and Illness*, *Mindfulness for Health*, and *Mindfulness for Women*.

Introduction

People will tell you they want a cure, but really, they just want pain relief.[1]

When I was thinking about my motivation for writing this book, I remembered a discourse in the early Buddhist literature that features a conversation between the Buddha and one of his disciples, Mahānāma. Mahānāma is somewhat confused about pleasure and happiness, and wonders 'who lives in greater pleasure' – a king or the Buddha? The king in question, Bimbisāra, was a patron, lay follower, and friend of the Buddha. With a little latitude, I've imagined a conversation between King Bimbisāra and the Buddha on one of their occasional meetings.

In this meeting, Bimbisāra remarks that he must be happier than the Buddha. After all, he has everything he could possibly desire, including his palaces and jewels, his wives and attendants, his dancing girls, elephants, and horse-drawn chariots. In comparison, the Buddha has so little, in fact, almost nothing. The Buddha has a spare robe and his begging bowl, and access to simple medicine, but he has no security even as to where his next meal is coming from or where he will sleep that night.

The Buddha doesn't refute Bimbisāra's assertion that his wealth and power confer greater happiness, but instead he asks a series of questions. He asks the king if he could sit alone, without any of his precious items or his attendants fulfilling his every wish, for just one hour and be happy and content. Bimbisāra doesn't need to think and he quite confidently says, yes, he could. The Buddha then says, 'Forget one hour, what about the whole day'? Bimbisāra really thinks about this – the joys of good food, soft couches, and dancing girls – and he is clearly less certain, but eventually he says, yes, he could sit alone all day and remain happy. Then the Buddha extends the period to one week, and the king knows his limits. No, he says, he couldn't sit alone for a week and remain happy. I imagine Bimbisāra looking slightly abashed and saying he would actually be quite miserable.

The Buddha, by contrast, was confident that he could remain content sitting on a riverbank or under a tree, day after day. The Buddha's happiness was intrinsic to his mind rather than dependent on pleasant things happening to him. This is expressed very beautifully in the *Karaṇīya Mettā Sutta*, the Buddha's discourse on loving kindness, which expresses the wish for others, 'may they be those whose self is happiness'. *In their essence* they are happy, not because of having a good day, even a series of very good days!

This story raises some questions. What is happiness? What makes us happy? Are we seeking happiness in the right places? And, looking back to the quote at the beginning of this introduction, do we know the difference between the happiness of 'pain relief' and the longer-lasting satisfaction of the 'cure'?

I, like many people, often feel very happy in nature. I remember one holiday in Crete, with long hiking days and stopping in remote village squares, or on rocky outcrops with fantastic high mountain views, for lunch. We would ravenously consume a picnic of, by now, slightly dry crusty bread, locally grown tomatoes, olives, and a bit of strong-tasting goats' cheese, washed down with spring water (and I mean water from an actual spring rather than the specially bottled and carbonated stuff). It was delicious. It was a perfect day!

There is another type of happiness that comes, the Buddha says, from the quality of our minds. We can make a distinction between happiness that is dependent on sense experiences which will come and go, and happiness that comes from the inner quality of a mind that dwells in such states as love, equanimity, and wisdom.

A mind and heart where appreciation, gratitude, and love are frequent visitors will be a happy mind. A mind that is angry or habitually disgruntled does not feel good and will find itself increasingly unhappy. A compulsive Internet surfing habit may appear to bring enjoyment and satisfaction but when we look more closely at the quality of heart, there can be a grasping which feels tight and contracted in the body and mind.

I appreciate the stark simplicity of Anthony de Mello's words quoted at the beginning of this chapter. He questions our motivation to practise the Dharma, the Buddha's teachings. Is our motivation to alleviate our immediate pain and have a pleasant life, or do we want the full cure from the suffering of delusion and selfishness? In other words, are we motivated by pleasure or by wisdom? If I take the words as a helpful mirror, to be held up in any moment of awareness, they show me where I'm at, and how far there still is to go.

Often, our happiness is the result of pleasant and enjoyable experiences which feed our senses and lift our mood. This includes meditation, which can give rise to joyful and calm states of mind. All these states relieve our suffering and open our hearts, which is lovely. But how do we react when something unpleasant comes along, as it inevitably does in the ups and downs of life? The degree of equanimity and acceptance in our response tells us a lot about how we are relating to pleasure in our lives, and whether we have become attached to having it.

One of the fruits of meditation practice and, particularly, mindfulness practice, is that we can experience colours, sounds, sights, smells, and tastes more vividly, and this in itself is often very pleasant. It's as if we are living up close to our lives rather than through a haze some distance away. But it is important to be clear that this pleasure and the happiness arising is a by-product of practice rather than the end goal. Practice can take us much further than delighting in and grasping after sense experiences, and this is what the Buddha was pointing to with King Bimbisāra. When we meditate, our sense faculties will naturally be heightened, but how do we use that temporary happiness and appreciation in the mind to deepen towards wisdom?

Much of what we will explore in this book will be concerned with developing a quality of mind that makes us truly happy and frees us from mental suffering. In particular, we will look at how to cultivate mindfulness and wisdom, which I'll often talk about as Right View. The Buddha, sitting alone on a riverbank, or in a grove of trees, was able to remain there not because he was blissed out in nature, though he may well have had some appreciation of the beauty of his surroundings, but because of the wisdom in his mind and heart that gave him a clear understanding of the causes of suffering and happiness.

A Personal Journey

This book has come out of my own personal practice. It is a journey that started thirty-five years ago when I first learned to meditate at the Triratna Centre in East London. As journeys do, it has covered much ground during these years. One of my difficulties early on in practice was a tendency to try too hard in meditation and become tense, which led to lots of frustration which, of course, produced more tension. In addition, I was often meditating in quite a lot of pain due to the regular migraines I have had since I was a child. During formal periods of meditation, I found myself doing less and less to avoid the vicious circle of escalating tension and pain. Although 'just sitting' in an unstructured way was helpful, I couldn't quite escape the feeling that there was more I could be learning.

A significant crossroad came twenty years ago when I started to practise more intensively with the *Satipaṭṭhāna Sutta*, the Buddha's discourse whose title means 'being present with mindfulness' or 'attending with mindfulness'. The Buddha teaches us to be present to four fields of experience: body, feeling, mind, and the Dharma. While there are many ways to practise using the *Satipaṭṭhāna Sutta*, I came across one that emphasized receptivity to experience combined with an approach to insight. I have been following this particular path in practice ever since. The feeling that I could be doing more was gradually resolved through a practice I describe as 'watching the mind', or a coming together of receptive mindfulness and wisdom.

For many years now I've been deepening my own practice of mindfulness and wisdom and sharing what I've learned though leading retreats. This book has come out of my own explorations in personal practice as well as through the many experiences described, comments offered, and questions asked by retreatants.

The group dialogues on retreats, where retreatants articulate their own experiences and questions in relation to the practice, are often my favourite part of the daily schedule. Exploring and answering these questions helps me find the words to describe my own experiences, and understandings of the practice, and then to share them with others.

My explorations into the *Satipaṭṭhāna Sutta* came first through books and then through attending many retreats with *Satipaṭṭhāna* specialists. Practising under their guidance helped me view the *Satipaṭṭhāna Sutta* not just as a fascinating teaching, but as a map of the mind within which I could locate meditative experiences and understandings.

I have had the great fortune to practise with some wonderful teachers and I want to mention the two most significant to whom I'm incredibly grateful.

From the earliest days of my Dharma life, Sangharakshita, the founder of Triratna, was my primary teacher. His breadth of Dharma knowledge and clear wisdom, along with his unparalleled vision for Sangha, has given me a context in which to live a life of meaning and depth, surrounded by Dharma friends and practitioners. The people I've lived and worked with or been on retreats with over the years have all deepened my sense of what it is to live a Dharma life.

Sangharakshita taught me how to think intelligently and not take things at face value. He emphasized that each person's spiritual path may look a little different, and, in a typically mischievous comment, he quipped that we are not sheep being driven along the same path yearning to stray off towards some succulent grassy verge!

> There is no question of forcing yourself to follow a
> particular track or go in a particular direction. The path
> simply represents the individual solution to your own
> particular predicament.[2]

Almost by chance, while I was seeking good conditions for a long (and inexpensive) retreat, Sayadaw U Tejaniya in Burma (now known as Myanmar) was recommended to me. While being very strong on mindfulness, his approach particularly prioritizes Right View –

recognizing the importance of a Dharma perspective in whatever one is doing. This potent combination of mindfulness and wisdom has helped me to find a strong insight dimension to meditation.

Since meeting U Tejaniya in 2007, I have spent a total of a year and a half on retreat with him in Myanmar and within Europe. He has a real gift for communicating what he has learned through the practice of watching the mind with awareness and wisdom. His own mind is delightfully lively and curious, irreverent, wise, and deeply steeped in the Dharma. His own past mental suffering informs his compassion and humour.

A slightly inelegant analogy sums up my relationship to these two great teachers. Sangharakshita's teaching is like a big cake, whole and complete. My life is lived within it – and made sense of – through it. And U Tejaniya's teaching is a particularly rich and deep slice of that Dharma cake. It doesn't profess to be the whole cake and yet I find it essential and central to my particular path to insight.

I see many differences but also similarities between these two spiritual teachers and, although they never had the chance to meet, I like to think that they would have got on. In my imagination, I see them connecting through an unerring commitment to the *spirit* of the Dharma and a willingness to jettison the *letter* when not required.

How to Use This Book

The eight chapters in the book will introduce you fully to a model of mind and a way of working with mindfulness and a Right View Dharma perspective. It is primarily intended as a practical guide to working with your mind in a gentle though incisive and insightful way, always guiding you towards your direct experience of body, heart, and mind. The book aims to guide you from a simple mindfulness practice through to watching the mind steadily with awareness and wisdom, as a natural expression of your being. Each chapter introduces a different aspect of experience and builds up the practice to include awareness of more subtle dimensions of the body and mind.

In addition to the chapters you will find *Mindful Pauses, Mindful Life Moments*, and *Led Meditations*.

Mindful Pauses. Throughout the book are various exercises that help you to explore more experientially the ideas within each chapter. I've called these 'mindful pauses'. They will help you get a sense of the different aspects of body and mind by highlighting them individually. For instance, there is an exercise inviting you to explore the difference between *being mindful* of your direct experience and *thinking about* your experience. The 'mindful pauses' encourage you to explore how you are practising being aware during formal periods of meditation and off the cushion so as to cultivate continuity of mindfulness.

Mindful Life Moments. Usually situated in between one chapter and the next, there is a short piece drawn from my own life and practice. These are taken from my blog to give you a sense of the practice as it is lived out through my life and to demonstrate how it can be lived out in your own life. You might be surprised to see how many of these 'mindful life' episodes take place far away from the meditation cushion and formal practice. The nature of this practice is well suited to be carried into all aspects of your life with an emphasis on a quality of awareness that can be present wherever we are and whatever we're doing.

Often, these mindful life pieces come from ordinary moments like visiting the dentist or being at a funeral or supermarket shopping. Or I might write a blog when my interest is caught by something I've been reading. That then morphs into a practice reflection that impacts on my experience of mindfulness and wisdom.

Led Meditations. I've included a link to several led meditations to support your own formal meditation practice. They mirror the chapters, in that the practices introduced in each meditation progress from initially quite simple grounding exercises to more complex and subtle aspects of experience. Over the course of the book we'll build up the practice to include different dimensions of experience, filling in more features in the landscape of the mind. The penultimate led meditation brings the whole practice together.

Why Practise in This Way?

> This is the direct path for the purification of beings,
> for the surmounting of sorrow and lamentation, for
> the disappearance of dukkha and discontent, for the
> realisation of Nirvana, namely the four satipaṭṭhānas.[3]

The 'sales pitch' from the Buddha, in the opening words of the *Satipaṭṭhāna Sutta*, is that it is a direct path to Enlightenment or Awakening. It cuts to the chase through its focus on directly knowing and being mindful of whatever is happening in our experience. There has been an explosion of different applications of mindfulness in the past fifteen years in the West. Mindfulness is so ubiquitous you could ask almost anyone hanging out on a street corner what mindfulness is and they would have some idea. They might say practising mindfulness makes you calm, or be present, or relaxed – and none of those would be wrong.

And yet, the Buddha says practising the *Satipaṭṭhāna Sutta* is a direct route to Awakening, the goal of spiritual practice. It is clearly so much more than having the benefits of a calm and relaxed mind, important though they are. What makes the difference is when mindfulness and wisdom are brought together. There is a lovely word in the Pali language spoken at the time of the Buddha: *sati-paññā* which means awareness + wisdom. The *sutta* is saying that the practice of mindfulness is not enough to take us all the way, that wisdom is an essential perspective which we train our mind in so it informs the way we view our experience.

Many meditation practices and approaches can be drawn from the *Satipaṭṭhāna Sutta*'s few hundred lines. There are meditation methods using noting techniques, or to forge strong concentration. Some practices focus on body sensations, or on repeatedly scanning the feeling tone throughout the body. Yet others focus on the mind that is observing all that is happening.

The approach I've been taught, and am taking in this book, is one that takes the mind itself as the object of investigation. I'm presenting the Buddha's teaching from the *Satipaṭṭhāna Sutta*, essentialized down to Awareness (or mindfulness) and Right View (a wisdom perspective).

According to Sangharakshita, 'We should be watching our minds all the time.' We probably know this, but we might have a question as to *how*, exactly? This book is my attempt to answer that question.

Sometimes when we try to be more mindful, we can start feeling a bit artificial or stiff. In this book, I try to point to an awareness that feels open, flexible, and 'uncontrived'. Uncontrived mindfulness doesn't feel 'added on' to experience but takes in, in a very natural way, just what is happening. The uncontrived aware mind is receptive, curious, and open. It works in tandem with the qualities of the wisdom mind such as clear seeing and equanimity. The uncontrived mind sees things as they really are, with spaciousness and clarity.

There is another motivational pitch in the words the Buddha leaves us with at the end of the discourse. Not content with just giving his audience the teaching, he wants to end with a bang. His strong exhortation in the final words of the *sutta* leaves us in no doubt as to the potential of practising in this way.

Speaking to the monastics and townsfolk of Kammāsadhamma in northern India 2,500 years ago, the Buddha describes the fruits of practising the *Satipaṭṭhāna Sutta* diligently, and with discernment. Those fruits, he says, are a high degree of spiritual realization leading to the end of suffering, leaving in its place a mind full of the happiness of peace. Moreover, he stresses that all these fruits can be attained, not in some distant future, not even

> seven years ... six years ... five years ... four years ...
> three years ... two years ... one year ... seven months
> ... six months ... five months ... four months ... three
> months ... two months ... one month ... half a month
> ... if anyone should develop these four satipaṭṭhānas in
> such a way for seven days (these fruits can be expected)[4]

Because King Bimbisāra was dependent on sense enjoyments for his happiness, he was vulnerable to suffering when he lost them. The

Buddha, content to be with things just as they were, no longer clung to anything, and so he was free from the mental suffering inherent in holding on to fleeting pleasures of the senses.

The key to ending suffering is not about whether we have lovely things or joyful experiences, but how much we cling to them. We all cling and hold on to what we love and what we want, as well as what causes us suffering. And we can all learn not to cling, and therefore not to suffer. This is the radical reorientation of practice. An important part of the process is to see the key role awareness and wisdom play in ending suffering. We see in our own direct experience what makes the mind suffer and what makes it happy and free from suffering. When the mind really understands this, there is no contest. It is like holding a hot coal – when we realize what is causing us pain, we drop it.

This is what I want to share with you in the following pages. I want to share my personal journey and make it accessible to you and the particularities of your own practice. I hope to communicate what I've learned from many years of skilled and generous guidance, and the many years of moment-by-moment mindfulness practice.

Chapter one

The Natural State of Awareness

Awareness is revolutionary.[1]

Why Be Aware?

To be aware, we must want to be aware. This sounds obvious, but if we don't understand the value of mindfulness, and therefore of cultivating and encouraging it, our motivation will founder. It helps to have a clear intention to practise and to nourish the intention through reminding ourselves of why it is important to be aware. In the story about King Bimbisāra, I made a distinction between happiness that comes from various pleasures of the senses, and the happiness produced by the quality of the mind free from clinging.

Mindfulness, or awareness, is key to recognizing the difference between mind states that lead us towards suffering, or to freedom and happiness, in each moment of our lives. The shift of perspective from relying on externals for our happiness to realizing we can develop our internal world makes awareness even more significant. Usually we live our lives looking through the mind to the world. We tend to relate to the beauty of a sunny day, rather than the beauty of the mind that is happily knowing it. We invest more of our attention in *what we are aware of* than in the *quality of the mind that is aware*.

In this practice, we use mindfulness to watch the mind directly rather than the 'objects' of experience. Although it sounds simple, it is not easy, so, in one way or another, I'll be spending much of the book talking about it.

What brought me to meditation was exactly this shift from external to internal. I was twenty-three years old and searching for meaning. For the previous three years I'd travelled and hitchhiked through Australasia. Sometimes I slept rough – under a road bridge, on a church pew, even in a beachside public toilet. Travelling felt too safe, so I toyed with blowing my remaining few hundred dollars on a week in a posh hotel so I could experience what it felt like to remove even this modest security net. I was seeking adventure, but even though I saw much beauty on my travels I experienced a lot of loneliness and boredom. In the last nine months, I fell in love with skydiving and, despite a near-death experience (of the not being able to find my ripcord kind), I continued 'jumping' once I got home. Temporarily living in London, I followed up on an intention formed in Southeast Asia, to learn to meditate. Typically, rather than trying out a class or two, I threw my adrenalized, restless, searching self into a six-day retreat.

There were many wonderful and scarily new things during the retreat, including meeting others who felt as passionate as me but were less confused! The one revelation that beat all the rest was that my inner world could be as meaningful, if not more so, than the outer one. All that seeking of novelty, excitement, and beauty could be directed towards knowing what was happening within my own heart and mind. I learned that the quality of my response to the world was an unknown continent that meditation enabled me to explore. I learned how automatic it was for the mind to reach outwards, grasping new sources of stimulation, but how restful it was to settle back and let the mind be aware of itself.

We underestimate the value of mindfulness if we simply use it to be aware of the world through our senses. It becomes a tool of immense value when used to watch the mind, allowing the quality of the mind to change for the better through sympathetic and discerning observation. The adventure of awareness is revealed though understanding which types of thoughts and actions lead to suffering, and which ones don't. As Sangharakshita says in the short aphorism at the beginning of the chapter, awareness is revolutionary. To be able to attend to our inner processes, rather than act out of them, changes everything.

The Natural Mind

Awareness is as natural to us as breathing. As living, feeling, sensing human beings we have the ability to be aware, not only of ourselves, but aware of others and the world we share. We can be aware through our physical senses which give us access to the external world with all its beauty and ugliness and all that is in between, as well as our inner worlds of thoughts, imagination, and much more. We hear a bird singing, or a car starting up, or a dog barking, without any effort at all. The sound might be somewhere in the background of our experience, or more immediately in the foreground. We might barely know it is happening and it registers slowly in our consciousness, or we're fully aware of it as soon as it happens.

As human beings we are naturally aware, but we can also take this process a step further through our innate reflexive consciousness: we can *know* that we're aware. This is what we can call a meditative awareness; we know that we know. As you are reading this book and probably sitting, or perhaps lying down, you can know that you are reading or sitting. We don't have to try to do this, but we can notice the process of becoming aware. It doesn't take a lot of effort; it's a subtle switch of consciousness that moves us from unawareness to awareness. There is a tiny inner gesture and then we *know* that we're moving or thinking or seeing. As well as being aware of the 'objects' of awareness – the dog bark or the car starting up – *we also know* we're aware of them. The mind registers sounds, sights, or touches, and awareness recognizes them.

Whether you're relatively new to meditation, or whether you've had a regular practice for many years, awareness or mindfulness often feels challenging. We sometimes talk of 'basic' mindfulness but really there is nothing basic or elementary about mindfulness. Whilst awareness is natural to the mind, it is a challenge to *remember* to be aware, to remember that mindfulness is always accessible when we stand still in the present moment. Most of the time we don't recognize the time travelling continually happening in our minds: we zip into the future with our planning minds, anticipating pleasures or difficulties, rehearsing imagined conversations, or we crash back into the past into painful memories or playing out old habits through our thinking patterns. We are often lost in the inner landscapes of our own minds. We almost never come fresh to the moment as it is happening right now. This is the challenge of mindfulness: to be here, now.

> *Lost*
>
> *Stand still.*
> *The trees ahead and bushes beside you*
> *Are not lost. Wherever you are is called 'here'*
> *And you must treat it as a powerful stranger,*
> *Must ask permission to know it and be known.*
> *The forest breathes. Listen, it answers,*
> *I have made this place around you,*
> *If you leave it you may come back again,*
> *Saying Here.*
> *No two trees are the same to Raven.*
> *No two branches are the same to Wren.*
> *If what a tree or a bush does is lost on you,*
> *You are surely lost. Stand still,*
> *The forest knows*
> *Where you are*
> *You must let it find you.*[2]

Here, in these words, is the receptive quality of awareness: we can let it find us if we stand still; if we stand still in the midst of the mind that is rushing in many directions at the same time and simply listen into or feel the quality of awareness in us. We must be patient with the rushing mind, allowing it to come to stillness in its own time. Once we notice the 'inner gesture' I mentioned above, then we are already 'Here', present and aware, and some aspect of our experience will be known to us.

From the examples above we can see that mindfulness is not something that happens only in formal practice. Certainly, spending some time each day meditating is vital to help the mind stabilize in the present moment, but we won't see many benefits from our mindfulness practice if we don't take practice 'off the cushion'. The Buddha, in the *Satipaṭṭhāna Sutta*, recommends mindfulness in all four postures of sitting, standing, walking, and lying down, as well as throughout our daily activities and during periods of silence and of talking. There is not a lot of wiggle room here! I take the Buddha to be saying 'be mindful continuously', and to do this we need a quality of awareness that is sustainable through different types of activities and mental states.

I want to communicate how mindfulness as a meditation practice, and awareness throughout the rest of our lives, can be one seamless, deepening 'knowing'. It is possible to learn as much, or more, 'off' the cushion, as when we're on it. While this takes a certain amount of application, the right information, and some skill, the main thrust of the practice is noticing what is already there when we're in the present moment. This doesn't demand special conditions but simple observation of the mind and body in their natural state, as they go about their work of binding our thoughts, feelings, perceptions, and sense experiences into the whole we call 'self'.

The Bigger Picture

As I was saying earlier, mindfulness has become increasingly familiar outside of Buddhist contexts over the past decades and is synonymous with a range of associations such as being in the present, being calm, and non-judgemental. The goal is usually to reduce suffering and to improve the quality of life. Within the Buddhist tradition, however, mindfulness has strong resonances with the wisdom mind, and the place of mindfulness is within the context of the Buddha's quest for Enlightenment, 2,500 years ago. The goal is nothing less than the end of suffering and complete freedom of heart and mind – the goal I'm concerned with in this book.

While awareness or mindfulness is of crucial importance, and in fact we can't get out of the starting block of spiritual practice without it, there is another factor of equal importance. This is Right View, or a wisdom perspective. Right View is not so much a specific view, but a way of observing what is happening in the mind, where the mind feels free of the usual habits of looking. Another way that we can talk about Right View is as a Dharma perspective that we hold at the back of the mind. To the extent that we have read or studied the Buddha's teachings, we have some access to his perspective. The teachings reinforce, from different angles, a perspective that enables mental spaciousness and clarity, and openness of heart.

The perspective of Right View is crucial when we are working on our minds in meditation. Lama Tilmann, from the Kagyu Tibetan lineage, talks of how in their tradition they don't encourage students to do intensive meditation training without input or feedback from the teacher. The teacher's role is to reorientate students to Right View, to keep mirroring back the wisdom perspective of the Buddha. Without this regular checking in on what is happening in their meditation, the student could well be reinforcing habitual views or perspectives rather than Right View.

The habitual view or attitude in the mind might manifest as boredom in meditation, or the attitude of wanting to get meditation over and done with before doing other, more enjoyable things. Or we might be trying hard to reach some of the exotic meditative states we've heard other people talk about. All these attitudes are probably familiar to us in our daily lives, so it is not surprising that they get transferred easily to our meditation, or that we don't always recognize how they are influencing our practice.

Right View can be compared to a navigational aid that helps ships at sea maintain their course rather than veering off a few degrees. For the first few miles, an error of a degree or two won't make much difference, but over a journey of a thousand miles, the ship will end up way off course. And in the ocean, without landmarks, it becomes impossible to see how far you've gone from your destination. In meditation, the Dharma perspective is both the map that allows us to recognize where we are, and where we're headed, and the compass that guides our journey.

Whether we are guided by a teacher, or the information we take in from reading books, Dharma study groups, or listening to podcasts, eventually we need to develop our own internal guide. The Dharma perspective moves from being 'out there' to 'in here'. Then, we can recognize the signs of going off course and learn to sail the inner storms, rough seas, subtle currents, and fair winds. Right View becomes internalized and increasingly accessible to guide us to, as yet, unknown territories of wisdom.

While most of the material in the early chapters of the book will focus on exploring and establishing mindfulness, those chapters will be seeded with glimpses of the wisdom perspective. It is not until chapter 4 that we'll focus exclusively on Right View. But by the time we reach this chapter you will find you recognize and feel some familiarity with the wisdom perspective offered because of its close connection with aspects of mindfulness. Of course, you'll also bring your own previous experience to the practice of mindfulness; to whatever extent you have studied and practised the Dharma, those teachings will be working away at the back of your mind. They'll enable you to recognize the mental factors that are helpful in keeping you on course, and those that steer you into treacherous waters.

In the rest of this chapter, I'll offer some broad ideas that can be helpful to get a flavour of the practice of mindfulness when working with Right View.

What's in a Word?

You'll see I'm using the words 'mindfulness' and 'awareness' interchangeably. Does it matter if you say one or the other? No, not really. Sometimes, as in the next chapter, I'll talk more about mindfulness as the Buddha defines 'Right Mindfulness' – that is, mindfulness in its fullest sense working with a variety of supporting qualities. At other times, I'll talk more about awareness, which perhaps has other associations such as receptivity. Many times, I'll use both words in the same sentence, along with others that bring out the multifaceted nature of the jewel of mindfulness.

At its heart, mindfulness is simply 'knowing'. Often, we know things in a *University Challenge* sort of way; we store up facts to rattle them off at the appropriate moment. And while this is impressive and useful at times, in meditation we are not talking about intellectual knowing. Mindful knowing is about feeling and sensing what is happening, as it happens in the present moment. There are other words we can use to describe how we know things are: we can *notice* something, we can *pay attention*, as well as *be aware*. We can also *bear something in mind* or *be conscious of* something. All these words help us build up a sense of the experience of awareness or mindfulness.

The words we use are important because they point to the *experience* of what it is to be aware. The experience of the realization of the Buddha's teachings is often said to be indescribable, because we can't use concepts to share the experience itself. There is a well-loved image in the Buddhist tradition of a finger pointing at the far-off moon to describe the relationship between the teachings (the finger) and the understanding or experience (the moon). It is important we don't mistake our concepts and ideas about the Dharma for the direct experience of wisdom. We can say the same for awareness. The various words used to say what mindfulness is are all fingers pointing to the *experience* of being aware.

Let's try an exercise to connect with awareness in the present moment.

Mindful Pause: Coming to Awareness

Settle back in a comfortable chair. You can be inside, or outside if it's warm enough. Your eyes can be open or shut. If the eyes are open, let your gaze be soft without looking at anything directly.

You're not trying to pay attention to anything in particular but allowing yourself to come to rest. Notice moments where you know you're present and aware. You're not trying to make these present moments happen but enjoy them when they're there.

Have the attitude that there's nothing to do but notice these moments of presence in a relaxed and open way.

Keeping this attitude, allow yourself to see what your mind is knowing in these moments.

You might be aware of sounds around you, or different sensations in the body. Or the sensations of the breath as it moves with the inhalations and exhalations, and the spaces in between, awareness of the living breath.

You might notice how your attention moves between different types of objects. For example, firstly the breath, and then sounds, and then the warmth of your hands, and then a thought.

You can be gently awake to the movements of awareness, as it takes in different objects.

Every now and again just check you are present, and relaxed, and resting in the moment.

Sit like this for as little as 5 minutes or as much as an hour.

'Thinking About' and 'Being Aware'

Let's continue to explore the territory between 'the finger' and 'the moon'. Other ways this dichotomy is expressed is through 'concept' and 'direct experience', or 'thinking about' and 'being aware'. It's worth giving this area more consideration as the thinking or conceptualizing mind is so dominant for most of us. It was not for nothing that Descartes said, 'I think, therefore I am'. What an influence those words, calling down from the seventeenth century, have had on our world and our experience! Our thoughts and ideas are usually the lens through which we experience everything else, which can lead us to become cut off from a broader, more expansive way of being.

This is not to deny how necessary the thinking faculty is to us. We can do very little without it, but we tend to overuse it and allow it to reign over other faculties, completely dominating how we engage with the world, and ourselves within it. The thinking faculty is not the whole of the mind, but just one faculty or capacity within it. Awareness, with its capacity for 'knowing' or 'noticing', is another, and if we can shift the balance more towards *being with* experience, and spend less time *thinking about* it, we will find awareness more accessible and our experience of ourselves more relaxed and balanced.

As a teacher, I frequently hear students in the early years of meditation describing how they were 'thinking about the breath' rather than 'being aware of breath sensations', for example. We need to be patient with ourselves in this process of reorientation towards a mode of noticing feeling and sensation, rather than jumping straight to ideas and concepts. We do this by tuning into what is happening in our actual experience. This is often more simple, subtle, and restful than all the opinions, attitudes, and views embedded in our conceptual mode of being.

One of the main 'enhancers' of the thinking mind is the tendency of the mind to proliferate. Words quickly breed more words; one little idea can spawn many others, each with its cascade of images, memories, imagined futures, and more words. Before we know it, the mind can feel full of thoughts. Other contributors to the proliferating mind are the feelings and emotions generated by our thoughts. For

Uncontrived Mindfulness

example, if we have a thought that we're getting ill, we may feel anxious. This in turn may produce thoughts tinged with anxiety, such as being worried we won't be able to meet our responsibilities if we're sick, or that we might lose our job. If we allow the thoughts to continue unchecked, the anxiety may well increase into a spiral, leaving little room for awareness in the mind.

Proliferation happens just as easily with thoughts we find pleasant. Here we are more likely to be lost in a swirl of thinking that reinforces the enjoyment we're getting from the thoughts, perhaps by reliving a compliment we've been given, and imagining what it might lead to. Someone might 'like' something I've written, and, if allowed free reign, before I know it I'm on an imagined best-seller list. Thinking is very seductive and pulls us into a vortex of increasing intensity, but with awareness we can learn to attend to the process of thinking, rather than the story or content of the thoughts.

Thoughts and thinking are like a hot air balloon that is pulling away from the earth, always wanting to take flight. Mindfulness is more in touch with the element of earth and the feeling of 'grounding'.

When we're more aware of what is happening directly in our experience, we notice details that we usually skim over. When we're aware of the process of breathing, for example, we can tune into what breathing feels like: there will be various sensations in different parts of the chest, abdomen, and throat, some movement of contraction and expansion, and we may notice the temperature changing between the coolness of the air on the in breath and the warmth of the breath we exhale. There are any number of different types of sensations we can notice, and we can also be aware of how they are constantly changing. Some sensations will be subtle and others obvious.

While noticing the breath sensations, it's likely that awareness will take in other things in the broader field of awareness. There might be tensions or tightness in certain parts of the body that have come about through sitting for a while, or you might recognize relaxation in the body, or in the mind. With awareness, we don't try to feel anything special, and we're not concerned if there seems to be little happening; we simply notice what is there to notice.

In meditation we'll most likely find ourselves moving between the two modes of mind, 'thinking about' and 'being aware', and this is natural. Gradually, with practice, we'll find the mind is able to rest more in awareness, and thinking will become simply one of the many things that happens in awareness. I will say more about this in chapter 6.

Mindful Pause: 'Thinking About' and 'Being Aware'

Take some time to be with your experience of the body. You might find the attention moves between objects of attention, such as the breath, or the sitting bones, or various other physical experiences. Let body and mind relax.

Feel into the experience of the sensations of the body. What do you notice? Before you even label the sensations pleasant or unpleasant, or describe such things as 'pressure' or 'heat' or 'softness' – how do the sensations feel?

Labelling perceptions may well come along with the direct experience of sensation, and that's fine; we're not trying to get rid of any aspect of experience, but to notice a fuller picture. If possible, give a bit more weight to the experience of sensation, and recognize that clearly.

When you notice a mental image or words going along with the sensations, know those too. For example, you might 'see' the breath going through the body, or automatically be naming the in and out breaths. Know these experiences as 'concept objects' or 'thinking about' experience, rather than the direct experience.

Often our experience will be a mixture of the two modes of being, but through greater relaxation and awareness we can rest more with the direct experience.

Any Object Will Do

In the long tradition of Buddhism, there are many approaches to meditation. They fulfil different purposes but have the same general aim of calming the mind enough to be able to engage in some type of insight practice. How *much* calm or stability is required is a question that has exercised meditators throughout two and a half millennia.

There are two main answers to this question. The first approach, which the Buddha called 'directed' attention (*paṇihita*) brings the mind to a point of stability, through attending to a single focus, such as the breath. Whenever we find our attention has wandered, we gently bring it back to this focus. Over time the mind becomes increasingly able to stay undistractedly with the chosen object, in this case the breath. With this type of practice, we usually need certain conditions for it to go well, such as a quiet environment, and enough time in sitting meditation to allow the stability of mind to build. The strength of directed practice is that it leads to powerful states of absorption and access to many of the higher states of consciousness the Buddha talked about.

The second approach to stabilizing the mind encourages the recognition of whatever objects of experience are present, such as the breath sensations, sounds, or thoughts, and uses them to stabilize awareness. The Buddha called this second type of cultivation of a stable mind 'undirected' (*apaṇihita*), which he linked to the practice of satipaṭṭhāna. Here we are not using any particular object to help focus the mind. This is the approach we'll be exploring in this book.

The key feature of the second, undirected, method is that instead of stabilizing attention on a *single* aspect of experience where the aim is for the mind to become absorbed in the object, we train awareness to use *any* object. Whatever is noticed becomes something that can help stabilize awareness. In this second approach, which I'll call 'receptive mindfulness', the mind doesn't need such deep stability as when we're working with a single object. In the words of the *Satipaṭṭhāna Sutta*, we need 'mindfulness established . . . to the extent necessary for bare knowledge and continuous mindfulness'.[3] We need just enough stability of mind to become more continuously aware of anything that is happening through any of the sense 'doors', including the mind – a sixth sense in Buddhist thought. We don't need the powerful concentration of directed attention which is more suited to absorption practice. We trade off that ability for a light and flexible attentiveness that allows us to observe whatever is happening as it happens.

In this type of practice the insight perspective is embedded right from the start with the instruction to establish mindfulness to the extent necessary *for bare knowledge.* We become aware of experiences passing through awareness in order to bring some degree of objectivity to our subjective experience. One of the strengths of this method is that it doesn't depend on a certain kind of inner 'weather', such as feeling relaxed or happy, or external conditions that are quiet and peaceful. Awareness is available in every moment, and an unpleasant sound or grumpy mind state can be observed in a similar way to the sensations of the breath, without getting so involved in the thoughts and the story.

What do I mean with the heading above, 'any object will do'? With a few exceptions, most of the time, in this practice, we are not directing the mind to any particular object. In the practice, there is no greater benefit in being aware of the breath than in opening to sounds or staying with a feeling tone. The object is not important. Sayadaw U Tejaniya likes to say that 'we are not looking to grow the object; we are looking to grow awareness'. We need to be clear that no one object is better than any other. We are looking to encourage awareness to be present more of the time and this is possible with *anything* the mind notices.

Letting the mind choose its own object can be tremendously freeing to help us relax into a natural state of awareness. A word of warning, though: it's also possible to spend many hours of meditation mooching in low-key distraction without quite recognizing that we're not really being mindful! Of course, there will be plenty of times when we're not aware, and we need to be patient with ourselves and recognize that we're practising to become more mindful. We are training the mind to be present, and to recognize 'mooching mind' or 'switched off' mind, however we describe it to ourselves.

There is, of course, some overlap between the two approaches I've outlined. Often, in the 'directed' method, before the attention comes fully to the single focus, it is helpful to give the mind space to settle. If we're too quick or insistent to focus, the mind is likely to rebel. And 'receptive mindfulness', particularly in the early part of formal sitting, can often benefit from periods where we anchor the mind in one aspect of experience such as body sensations to help stay present.

'Dedicate your life / to the twin and warring gods of Precision / and Wild Abandon', says the poet Emily Hasler.[4] The practice of mindfulness takes dedication and involves a delicate balance between the precision of attentiveness without being overly forceful and an ability to let the mind be natural; we have to abandon attempts to control where we think our attention should go, so opening to the quality of letting go.

Receptive to Whatever Is Happening

> Receptivity is the first requisite of the disciple, and of anyone who wants to learn anything. We can be anything else we like; we can be wicked, we can be stupid, we can be full of faults, we can back slide. In a sense, it doesn't matter. But we must be spiritually receptive: we have to be willing and ready to learn. When we know that we do not know, then everything is possible.[5]

As you're reading this, you can tune into your direct experience through any of the senses. There's no need to choose something to focus on; it's more that you can notice where the mind is already going. The mind will naturally notice things and move on to the next thing. Perhaps, as you read, you notice the feel of the book or device in your hands, and the way that your body is sitting and any discomfort in your position. You might notice the letters on the page, and the movement caused by the breath coming in and out of your body. The longer you're present, the more you'll notice in a relaxed and natural way.

At times, you might be surprised by your experience of being mindful. There can be moments when our preconceptions dissolve and we're with the actual experience, whether it's of 'touch' or 'seeing', or the overall experience of being a breathing, sensing being. It is the quality of receptivity working with present moment awareness that allows this to happen.

Receptivity is an important aspect of mindfulness. When we're receptive, our ideas about things are less dominant and we're more willing to notice just what's in our experience already. We let the mind relax back, as in a comfortable armchair. When the body and mind are relaxed we can notice any tendency in the mind to reach out towards experience.

One of my favourite places to cultivate this quality of awareness is when I'm listening to live music. An experience from a few years ago has stayed with me. I was at a classical concert near where I lived in Cambridge. The programme consisted of several composers and I wasn't very familiar with any of them. I'd tended to avoid them, thinking they weren't what I liked and enjoyed. Once the music began, I let my attention be quite soft and broad. I was aware of the audience around me, and the natural wood of the auditorium, and the thirty or so musicians on the low stage.

At times, I would close my eyes and attend to the sounds. While I listened, I could see my mind seeking melodies and chord combinations that it liked, and rejecting what it heard as unpleasant. I became interested in these responses and in watching what else the mind was doing. Watching the mind allowed me to take a step back into a different mode. I was aware of sounds in great variety of pitches, rhythms, tones, and volume. Individual instruments sounded, clear notes rising and falling in a vast and ever-changing aural cascade.

The 'tune' became less significant and the sense of a particular piece being played became secondary to these momentary 'arisings' of a roller coaster sound bath. The whole concert became fascinating and thrilling, though I also felt quite calm, just observing what was happening. I knew I still didn't particularly 'like' the music, but the criteria of personal likes and dislikes had diminished in importance and slid into the background of my experience. This event was quite eye opening in terms of how simple awareness could transform an experience.

What about *Mettā*?

Usually, at some point when I'm leading a retreat, someone will ask about the place of loving kindness, or *mettā* practice, within the *Satipaṭṭhāna Sutta*. Although the Buddha doesn't mention *mettā* directly in the *Satipaṭṭhāna Sutta*, my sense is that implicit within his words about mindfulness is an attitude of mind that is in complete harmony with loving kindness.

When we are receptive, we're able to *allow* whatever is present to be there. This ability to allow what is happening, without having some sort of agenda about what *should* be there, is deeply kind. We don't judge, struggle with, or complain about what has arisen. When we allow or accept what is happening this is not the end of the story; we're not saying that any state of mind is helpful to our practice. We're simply saying that we accept that it's already present. In this way of practising, we don't oppose what's happening, or immediately bring in its opposite, but recognize it clearly with a kindly, spacious awareness. There are many colours that make up the palette of *mettā* including such qualities as curiosity, patience, and openness as well as the quality of mind that we looked at above, receptivity.

If, in your practice of open receptive mindfulness, you find yourself in the grip of some difficult mind states, to which you would usually consciously bring loving kindness, I suggest you first pause. Then notice anything in the quality of your awareness that *already* has the flavour of *mettā*. Sometimes, in our desire to rid the mind of unpleasant or 'negative' states, we will reach to action too quickly. When we do this, we can underestimate the resources already within the mind. Even that act of pausing, and checking, is an expression of self-trust, another resource of kindness.

Other ways that *mettā* operates within the practice are more connected with the wisdom perspective, and we will touch on this as we progress through the book.

Always Aware of Something

When we're meditating and allowing the mind to notice objects of experience in its own time, sometimes we can feel that nothing much is happening. Or even that *nothing* is happening. When we start to think that nothing is happening, awareness switches off and the mind either gets bored and starts distracting itself, or we go to sleep. What can happen in those times is that there is nothing compelling enough to exert a strong pull on our attention. Our overstimulated brains are used to highly colourful and dynamic happenings, and when these settle down as we meditate, we can fail to notice the more neutral sense objects that are left.

We are always aware of something. The mind is set up to recognize an object of experience through one or more of the senses during every moment of consciousness. Awareness might not be switched on to a moment where, for example, on waking you know the feel of the bed underneath your body, but in some rudimentary way, consciousness is picking up on those sensations and you might recall them later. We are always experiencing something. The more we are aware in the present moment, the more we'll feel the truth of this.

When we feel an absence of experiences to know, it may be that practice is actually going quite well. Perhaps the mind has quietened down so there are fewer obvious objects, and we might be overlooking more subtle experiences such as the quality of calm or peacefulness in the mind.

Or it may be that we have an idea in the mind that is getting in the way of what is happening. We might have an unseen expectation that something better should be happening. Perhaps we think there should be more bliss in the mind, or fewer thoughts. These thoughts are expectations and when we are not aware of expectations in the mind, they can lead us to think there is something wrong with our practice. We are then more likely to try and change the experience in some way rather than watch the unfolding process without interfering with what's happening.

In the next chapter I will explore mindfulness in its fullest sense as 'Right Mindfulness', and go into some of the qualities that the Buddha saw as most helpful and supportive to strengthening awareness and forming a basis for wisdom.

Mindful Life Moment: (Guide Our Feet in) the Natural Way

This song, 'The Natural Way', by the alternative folk band Seize the Day comes to mind this morning. I'm thinking about meditation and what to write. How not much happened in practice yesterday and how more and more I'm OK with that. There is a new contentment with experience. The demand for it to be interesting or insightful has dropped. Sometimes it feels like the mind is drifting and getting a bit lost in mind scraps of mental flotsam and jetsam and I wonder if it's just a slightly pleasant dreamy state. But the contentment is undeniable. There is ease and spaciousness in a mind that doesn't need anything else to happen in the moment.

Ease and naturalness have long been cultivated and hard won in a mind that is much more conditioned towards striving, towards strained effort and seeking results. The tendency to 'fiddle' with my experience, to make it something 'better' or closer to the idea of what I think *should* happen, has been tamed with curiosity. 'Curbing' mind has been seen over and over coming in sharply and cutting through a renegade thought. It has gradually lost its brute force and urgency through being known in the aware mind.

I'm looking to see the mind in its natural state. The 'fiddling' or 'curbing' are antithetical to that. I see how they create suffering in the mind causing the tightening in my shoulders and beginnings of a headache. Attempting to control thoughts, images, and stories leads to suffering and creates tension. There's no need to 'let go' of these things: seeing them in awareness, knowing them for what they are, and being interested in the process is enough.

Like the naturalist studying nature, I'm looking to see what's happening rather than interfere with how the anthill community, or the mind, function. Through simple observation of the mind in its natural state, going about its 'work' of thinking, perceiving, planning, intending, fantasizing – to name just a few of its functions – a universe opens up.

It's not the universe of 'content' but one of process. Like nature for the naturalist, almost anything, even the weirdest and ugliest bugs, becomes interesting and a thing of beauty to be marvelled over. What does a thought feel like? How do I know I'm feeling? What is the difference between anger and sadness felt in the body? I'm not asking these questions for an answer but to allow interest in the direct experience to grow.

Chapter two

How We Are Aware

> Awareness alone is not enough. Having a desire to really
> understand what is going on is much more important
> than just trying to be aware. We practise mindfulness
> meditation because we want to understand.[1]

For several years, I lived near a part of the UK coast with a large
wetland area that was a protected nature reserve. Sometimes, during
a walk alongside the sea with a friend, we would stop and sit for a
while in one of the bird hides there. Often nothing much happened;
a few ducks crossed the water, or I'd see a couple of gulls with my
binoculars. Occasionally something more exciting, like a sleek, black
cormorant, would fly in, or what for the past ten minutes had looked
like a reed revealed itself as a long-billed, stick-legged grey heron.

All in all, it was not an exciting pastime! However, I enjoyed it
in quite a subtle, low-key way. Because we were hidden in the hide,
nature just went about her business without being aware of us, which
was fun. It also nicely illustrated that awareness isn't about the 'object'
– remember, the object is whatever the mind is recognizing, or aware
of. Whatever I'm looking at or noticing through any of my senses is
secondary to the quality of mind that is aware of it.

Something like a duck or a moorhen is ordinary to me. I've seen
thousands of them over my life and regard them as commonplace. I
know they might not seem ordinary to everyone – say an Eskimo or
a Tibetan, who had never have seen a duck before. In the same way,
I found the chipmunks that are common in the northeastern USA
entrancing, especially when they would take seeds from my hand
and stuff them into their fat little cheeks before disappearing into
a nearby hole in the ground. But what sitting in the hide watching

ordinary ducks showed me was that pleasure and satisfaction come from being aware. We don't need exciting objects or even a great variety of them. We can be aware of *whatever* is in our experience and known through our senses. This is enough to support the growth of awareness over time.

What Helps Us to Be Aware?

The Buddha often described four qualities that together define mindfulness in its fullest sense. They frequently occur together in the Pali canon, the oral teachings that form the earliest surviving written record of the Buddha's teachings. These four qualities are what make up Right Mindfulness, one of the eight factors of the Buddha's noble eightfold path. Taken together, the eightfold path lays out the path to awakening through every aspect of our lives. The most significant discourse where the four qualities defining Right Mindfulness appear is the *Satipaṭṭhāna Sutta*.

These qualities are important and make a difference to our meditation practice and how we work with our minds, not only because they help awareness to become stronger but also because they communicate a perspective that is crucial to the whole project: *how* we are aware. For us to be mindful of whatever is happening, our minds need to be fit for the purpose of being aware.

It is one thing to be aware when the mind is quiet, pliant, or peaceful, which is often the case when things are going well for us, but quite another to be aware during those times when there is much more agitation and emotion present – when we're angry or distressed about something, for example. It is easy, then, to be caught up in an inner narrative about how things are, or how we are, how rubbish our mind is, how we feel we're just not getting anything out of sitting, and so on.

What quality of mind do we need, to be able to experience turbulent emotions, loud, competing thoughts, or physical pain, without immediately trying to emotionally reject those things, or getting overwhelmed by them? Without, in effect, losing our mindfulness. The four aspects of Right Mindfulness are addressing this question.

These four qualities can be found back in the bird hide story I started with. We need to **be present and receptive** with a breadth of awareness or we'll miss things happening through our senses. We also need a quality of mind that is open and balanced rather than opposing what it takes in. If we are bored with ducks and drakes, it is because the mind has decided they aren't important and switches off. We need to **be clear** about what we're noticing in a relaxed and **curious** way that is mindful, not only of the 'objects' around us, but also of the quality of mind that is knowing it all. And we are looking for some ease and **contentment** which helps us rest back rather than bring strain to the body and mind through reaching out to experience. We're happy to sit there in the bird hide without a big, exciting event to entertain us; the mind is, for once, at ease with itself.

The words above are my own informal ways of describing the feel of the mind when we are aware. Let's go through these qualities under the headings the Buddha used and see how they contribute to a full sense of Right Mindfulness, an awareness that is capable of being aware of any object or state of mind. They are:

1. **Mindful**
2. **Clearly comprehending** or **clearly knowing**
3. **Diligent**
4. **Free from desires and discontent** (in regard to the world of sense experience)

1. Mindful (*Sati*)

The first quality is mindfulness itself. This might be a bit of a surprise, but it is a simple and direct quality that is different from the combined qualities. Mindfulness or awareness is a translation of the word *sati*. By itself *sati* is simple, present moment awareness; it is accessible to us any time we pause and let our attention rest with what is happening directly in our experience. It also helps us remember and recollect what has happened in the past, though it is doing so through assisting our memory, rather than being the same as remembering.

The mind that is receptive and relaxed

What allows us to rest with our experience in the moment is a mind that is receptive and able to notice what's happening in a relaxed way. When I'm teaching, I like to talk about relaxing *into* awareness. It is often said that mindfulness is not something we do in an active way, but is a way of being. This points us to a relaxed quality of mind that, although it is receptive, is not passive. We are combining relaxation with attentiveness which helps us feel more present and embodied. You are not switching off in the way you might do by relaxing in front of the television, or when you're trying to go to sleep. You are relaxed *with* awareness.

You can try it out just sitting here reading. Just let yourself relax into what you notice. You might be aware of different body sensations or your breath or the sounds around you. You can notice some of those things whilst also knowing that you are reading the words on this page. It doesn't really matter *what* you notice. You want to see if you get a sense of how being present to your experience happens more naturally and is more pleasurable when you relax into it.

In one of Aesop's fables, the sun and the wind challenge each other to a contest over who is the stronger. From their vantage point in the sky, they see a lone figure far below. He is walking and wearing a long coat. The challenge is to see which of them can get the man to take his coat off. The wind has the first attempt and he blows so strongly that leaves blow off the nearby trees and the man's coat flaps loudly and whips around him. This makes him wrap the coat tightly to his body. The wind gets tired and the sun takes a turn. The sun uses a lot less effort and simply does what comes naturally. It shines a warm glow and before long the man starts to feel a bit hot. He loosens his coat so that it swings free, and eventually he removes it and walks with it hanging over his arm.

The sun in this story symbolizes receptivity. Receptivity doesn't oppose what is happening but opens to it. Awareness is receptive, so it's a quality of mind that is open to whatever it observes. It is not trying to change what's happening or make it different in some way even if something is unpleasant or reflects badly on us, as when we feel criticized. And as you see in the fable, the gentle and receptive way was effective.

The mind without agenda

Give up to grace
The ocean takes care of each wave until it gets
to the shore[2]

Often when we try hard to make something happen, we are trying in the wrong way and it works against us. When we put in a lot of effort, we usually have an agenda about whatever it is we want to happen. Having an agenda means we are less open and receptive to what naturally presents itself. I'll talk more about the type of effort we need to practise mindfulness when we look at the third of these four qualities.

A good starting point for receptivity is that we're willing not to know. We don't try to figure the mind out as if it were a maths problem; we're open to the possibilities of that moment.

It is natural to have views and ideas about what we want to happen, and we will all have our own preferences as to the type of experiences we want to have. It's also natural that we generally want those experiences to be pleasant or satisfying, and to show ourselves in a good light. Often, we will go to great lengths to preserve a gratifying experience or protect ourselves from painful ones, and even with all that mental effort we're usually only partially successful at best!

With mindfulness practice, our goal is not the pursuit of pleasant experiences or the avoidance of painful ones. When pleasant enjoyable experiences occur, they are a by-product of practice and secondary to the aim of simply being aware. When *sati* is present, we're broadening out what we're willing to experience, regardless of our preferences.

Looking at the natural mind

Another aspect of this receptive mindfulness is that it doesn't interfere with what is happening. Awareness doesn't fiddle with or manipulate experience to make it more to our liking. A good analogy for this quality of non-interference is that of the naturalist. A naturalist works in the environment of his or her subjects – in nature. They look at the behaviour and lifestyle of tiny insects, animals, or marine life in their natural environment. I think it's one of the reasons we find wildlife programmes on TV so fascinating. (And perhaps why human 'reality' shows are so popular too!) We learn about the habits of beings who are very different from us, as they go about their lives in warrens, or anthills, or miles under the ocean.

Naturalists don't tend to look at their subjects in the artificial environs of a laboratory, because they learn less about them that way. In meditation, we want to see as much as we can to learn about the heart and mind. We're not looking to observe only 'Sunday best', but the full range of states of being.

Awareness becomes stronger through not shying away from certain mind states in order to prioritize others. True mindfulness is impartial and without agenda. It hasn't decided in advance what the outcome will be but is open to whatever it might find.

Remembering and recollecting

As I mentioned earlier, mindfulness also has an association with memory and recollection. I'll give you a sense of how present moment awareness and remembering work together. This is a very simple example, but we'll see later in the book how it has other applications with much greater significance.

On my first trip to Myanmar, I spent several months in a retreat centre unlike any centre I'd been to in the West. For a start, the cockroaches were enormous. And the black forest scorpion I encountered at 4am stumbling to early morning meditation, waving its claws at me, was the size of a large crab! The meditation centre is on the edge of the colourful and sprawling city of Yangon but the area directly bordering us was rural, with water buffalo pulling ploughs in the fields around us.

The dwellings in the nearby village were mainly constructed from large thick banana leaves and bamboo, the standard building materials in Myanmar. The concrete two-storey buildings of the meditation centre had only been recently built on the fields at the far end of the village. Each dormitory block in the centre housed twenty bedrooms over two floors with a communal bathroom with several showers, toilets, and cold-water wash basins. Nothing worked particularly well, and bits and pieces were often being replaced with whatever was to hand. The taps on the half dozen wash basins were all different shapes and sizes. Not only didn't they match but they didn't turn on and off in a consistent direction.

Often when I went to wash my hands, I would turn the tap one way and nothing happened (occasionally the whole tap would swivel round within its ceramic setting without any water coming out at all). Of course, on the second try the right way was obvious, and I was able to wash my hands. Because there were six basins, and often in use, I couldn't use the same one regularly, so I had twelve chances of getting it right or wrong each time I washed myself. There were too many variations to memorize, I thought, but when I recalled what I knew about awareness influencing memory I thought again.

The way mindfulness works in relation to memory is that if we are present to our experience as it happens, we will be able to remember something more clearly later on. That made complete sense to me, so I started checking whether I was present and aware in those moments when I approached the basin and turned on the tap. For the first few times it was as hit and miss as ever, but then I started to more reliably turn the tap the right way, so water came on the first time of trying.

Through being present while choosing a basin, I was aware of its location in relation to other basins and the whole bathroom. Then I was aware, through using either my left or right hand to turn the tap. Very quickly I developed a visceral body memory of which taps worked well and which way I needed to turn the tap to get water.

This is different from remembering things through habit. A friend of mine who thought she was quite mindful came to a realization, when she moved bedrooms in the Buddhist community she lived in. She kept losing her car keys and she realized that what she had taken previously for mindfulness was in fact just a habit. In her old room, she had always dropped her keys into a drawer near the door to the room, but her furniture was arranged differently in the new room and she couldn't do that.

When we rely on being present in each moment, rather than doing things on automatic pilot, we're able to adjust to changes more quickly because we are relying on our actual experience rather than simple repetition.

We draw on the memory aspect of mindfulness by reminding ourselves to be aware, to be present. Over time, this intention is strengthened and becomes more natural for the mind to be aware, and less reminding is required.

We need to avail ourselves of further qualities that work with awareness skilfully and that really allow it to flourish and strengthen, leading to happy, ethical and wise states. The second of these qualities is *sampajāna* or clearly knowing.

2. Clearly Comprehending or Clearly Knowing (*Sampajāna*)

The quality of mind that clearly knows or comprehends, emphasizes the element of *understanding* in mindfulness practice. It is the mind that is aware intelligently and with some degree of wisdom rather than acting blindly, as when we're on auto pilot. This second quality works with *sati* and they are often translated together as 'mindful and clearly knowing'. Without clear comprehension, we are looking (at our experience) but we don't fully register what we are seeing.

There is a whole spectrum of clearly knowing: for example, when we're simply aware of the sensations of the breath as we feel them in the chest, throat, or a tickle in the nose. At a deeper level of mindful knowing we are able to understand the *nature* of the breath. Here we comprehend, in quite a matter of fact but visceral way, that what we call the breath is not a 'thing' at all but many insubstantial and rapidly changing sensations and moments of experience.

Clear knowing ranges from a simple awareness to a deeper understanding that is more akin to wisdom. There are many different facets of this quality. In this section I will go into some aspects, while leaving others for later chapters.

Continuity of purpose

Perspective is key to *sampajāna*. We not only know what is happening, but we know how it fits in with our overall spiritual purpose and direction. The key aspect of this quality is 'continuity of purpose' which helps us to keep going and follow our intentions through. The purpose of a Buddhist life is to deepen in wisdom and compassion, and awareness is a cornerstone to enabling those goals.

Our purpose can be *macro* – in relation to the direction of our whole life and overall values – or *micro* – as when we are meditating and noticing momentary aspects of inner experience like the quality of a thought, or how a particular sensation feels in the body. Micro moments carry our intention to practise awareness.

Of course, continuity of purpose is also applicable to watching our minds with awareness throughout the day. By remembering our purpose, which includes our intention to be mindful, we'll more naturally remember to be aware.

The warp and the weft

An image might help here. When fabric is being woven on a loom, the threads are set up in long rows at right angles to each other. The 'warp' threads are held under tension whilst the 'weft' threads weave under and over the warp, eventually creating a tight-knit pattern. You can probably imagine that on, say, a bright tartan weave or a simple cotton cloth.

Awareness, and the mind that is clearly knowing or comprehending in a deeper way, are similarly held together. The weft threads that go over and under the warp are like present moment awareness which moves and changes direction as it recognizes new objects in experience. It needs to be flexible and responsive. The warp is more constant in its direction; this is akin to a continuity of purpose and applying a consistent perspective to what is 'known'.

It is not easy to act in a consistent way, especially one that is in line with our values – the things that really matter to us. We may be very clear that acting in a loving way with our friends and family is important to us, but we also find them irritating at times and can all too easily lose touch with our aspirations. We may place a high value on honesty or clarity and then find ourselves in situations where we fudge the issue or just don't know how to act for the best.

How often do we decide we are going to get up each morning early enough to have enough time to meditate before we leave for work, and not manage to do that? We have set the intention because we know that meditation really helps us throughout our day or helps us towards an overall goal of wisdom and compassion. But time and time again, we end up staying up late, which makes it difficult to get up with the alarm, or just prefer the warmth of our bed for an extra doze.

Even carrying through an intention – for example, not to eat cakes and sweet things in order to maintain a healthy weight – can be incredibly difficult and we can find ourselves rationalizing treats or special occasions, just because we feel we need cheering up.

Continuous awareness and knowing

Sampajāna is what helps us stay in touch with – and work with mindfulness to remember –what is most important and valuable to us. When we're present more of the time, awareness becomes more continuous and we have an overall sense of continuity of *attention* through time. A lack of continuity of awareness will contribute to a start/stop mindfulness where it is harder to build momentum in practice.

This quality gives a broader perspective on our experience that takes in different dimensions of time. It combines present moment knowing with a clear recollection of past moments through having been being present to them (as with my example of the bathroom taps in Myanmar). This influences future moments (where I turn the tap the correct way first time) in many smaller and larger ways.

When we have continuity of attention it becomes possible to have a continuity of *intention*. Our values and spiritual goals gather more positive weight because we're more able to do what we say we will. In effect we become more reliable, or, in Sangharakshita's words, our energy becomes integrated.

Sampajāna keeps a thread of meaning running through our lives, reminding us in many different ways of our spiritual direction. This thread of intention is often quite subtle and manifests in delicate ways, reminding us of our connection to a deeper way of living. This might be through our ethical practice, keeping up regular meditation, or an intention to stay aware of the body throughout the day.

Asking the question

A further aspect of *sampajāna* is clearly knowing whether an action (including a mental action) is beneficial to practice or is likely to hinder it. This is directly related, in a very practical way, to moment-to-moment awareness, whether we are formally meditating or carrying mindfulness through to life activities such as washing up or typing or facilitating a meeting.

You can ask yourself, 'What would be helpful to do now in my practice?' or 'What's needed now?' You can do this if you're sleepy or thinking a lot or when nothing seems to be happening. For example, you might notice in sitting meditation that you've started to slump a little, and your breathing has deepened but the mind has a pleasant fuzzy feel to it. You know from past experience that these are all signs of you becoming sleepy. Asking the question 'What would help now?' interrupts the gradual slide into unconsciousness. You don't try and oppose the mind as it is or to find an answer to the question. You simply ask the question to stimulate some interest in the mind to help it be with what is already there.

When curiosity and interest are in the mind it is harder for hindrances to meditation to take hold, which allows the positive and helpful qualities to grow. Curiosity is part of what objectifies your experience and is the beginning of wisdom in action. Through your interest you look at an experience from different angles rather than ignore it and try to carry on regardless.

These questions and other similar ones help keep the mind awake to what is happening. They keep the 'knowing' quality from switching off and being replaced with a superficial skimming over experience. It is also a way of stepping back from being lost within our experience and gaining a degree of perspective.

We can keep this 'knowing' active within a formal meditation sitting or when we're practising being aware in daily life, or when we're presented with a situation where we're not sure what to do or what a skilful response would be.

Later, I'll look at other actions that might lead from the 'what's needed?' question, but for now it is important to not immediately default to 'doing something'. We see what can happen simply through mindfulness and clear knowing.

Sometimes, clear knowing is talked about as the 'intelligence' aspect of mindfulness. This is not an intellectual intelligence but one that is thoughtful and willing to look afresh rather than jump to conclusions and make unconscious assumptions about what is happening. It is an intuitive mental searching which has both breadth and precision. It is the intelligence of a mind that is tuned to wakefulness whilst also carrying a quality of stillness and ease.

Can you mindfully rob a bank?

Sometimes, a criticism of mindfulness is a perceived lack of moral foundation, particularly in its secular manifestations. Mindfulness in its original Buddhist setting is taught clearly within an ethical framework of 'precepts' or training principles. But mindfulness in the full sense that we are looking at it in this chapter is also part of what allows us to *recognize* our skilful or unskilful actions.

When we are mindful, we notice the quality of mind preceding any action and we can notice the *intention* behind the action. Of course, sometimes we miss the moment before the action and, before we know it, we've spoken harshly or acted greedily. It is not too late to learn, as we can gain much from noticing the mind quality *after* the action. We can ask ourselves if the action or thought produces suffering in us, which could be quite mild, such as a vague feeling of guilt, or a very strong sense of regret. Alternatively, does the action conduce to an openness of heart and freedom from suffering?

Sangharakshita once contrasted 'true' mindfulness to someone robbing a bank. He said that you can have someone bending over a safe, trying to crack its code, or the lookout guy outside scanning the street for signs of the police, and in both cases, they are alert, and vigilant to their tasks. The safe cracker probably needs to be relaxed to some degree to be successful and he needs to have some skill. He may well feel some satisfaction because things are going well and he's about to become rich!

But, Sangharakshita said, this is not mindfulness (in the sense of *sati* and *sampajāna*). Whilst there is focus and concentration, the open, content mind that is simply able to observe is missing. When we want something badly, the mental factor of desire tends to become dominant in our experience. The task of mindfulness is to 'hold' other factors of mind such as craving without suppressing it or indulging by acting it out. As you can imagine, the bank robber is not inclined to simply be aware of the desire to rob the bank or get rich; he *wants* to act on his craving. It is the craving that is dominant in his mind rather than mindfulness.

In this scenario, desire is in the driving seat of the mind whereas what we want in our practice is for mindfulness to be driving, and if desire or craving is present, for it to be a passenger. The mind of the bank robber is significantly different to awareness in the full sense we're talking about here. We are cultivating a quality of mind that recognizes what's happening in the present moment and has a continuity of purpose with our deepest values, which presumably don't include getting rich from robbing banks. Mindfulness includes the calmness and clarity of mind that is able to assess what's best for us and also others. If we leave that job to craving, we will be pulled here and there by whatever desires are uppermost, without regard to our values and therefore what will make us happy. True mindfulness recognizes that an ethical intention will lead to happiness, and an unethical or unskilful one conduces to suffering.

It is not that being mindful means we never act on our craving – ask any experienced practitioner if that is the case for them! But it means we are less likely to act mind*less*ly on impulse. We have an opportunity to pause and take in a broader range of factors; even though our habits are strong, we have more choice. When awareness is present, perhaps we don't take that second slice of cake or let out the sarcastic comment we'll later regret.

Desire is not always unhelpful (or in Buddhist terms, unwholesome). Sometimes desire is pointing to something that would benefit us – like the desire to move my body when I've been sitting a while, which is helpful to prevent my joints stiffening up, or the desire to meditate to deepen awareness and wisdom in the mind. If we are mindful, we can notice the motivation in the mind steering us towards skilful or unskilful actions and with that information we have the potential to make wiser choices.

3. Diligent (*Ātāpī*)

Diligence can sound a little dry and over-responsible, but practised well it gives us great staying power. The mind that is diligent has persistence as a characteristic. When we persist, we don't give up; we keep on with our efforts even when we can't see benefits or results yet. Mindfulness that can keep going has a very even quality rather than great surges of effort followed by falling back exhausted.

When we are diligent we apply just enough effort to stay aware. It can be very helpful to have a clear knowing of what that 'just enough' energy feels like in our experience, otherwise we're likely to underestimate and find the mind drifts, or (more likely) overestimate what is needed and use force. You can try this out with a simple exercise.

Mindful Pause: Touching Hands

Sit quietly for a couple of minutes first and let yourself relax.

Then have the palms and fingers of both hands lightly touching. You can feel the contact between your fingertips and parts of your palms. If you like, you can move your hands slightly apart and then back together again, making and breaking the contact.

What do you notice happening there? You are probably aware of different sensations from the touching together of your hands. Perhaps there is some tingling or slight pressure or heat from the touch. Whatever it is, just notice it.

You don't need to try to be aware of all the sensations or to be aware of them continuously, but just see what you notice when you remember.

Now ask yourself how much energy it takes to be aware of the sensations where your palms and fingers touch. Give yourself a couple of minutes to notice what happens.

You'll probably find that it's almost effortless to know those sensations. If you're present and have primed the mind (through reading the exercise) towards your hands touching, you'll naturally be aware of some of the sensations there.

Using that same relaxed and present quality of awareness, notice other sensations in your physical experience, allowing awareness to become broader.

You might find your attention is drawn to different places in your body, sometimes in very quick succession: from your fingertips to a slight ache in your shoulders or your lips touching together, then your feet on the ground.

It doesn't really matter what you're aware of – the important thing is the relaxed and receptive quality of awareness. This happens when we're not trying too hard and using more effort than we need to.

Try spending a few minutes just being aware of different objects of experience that you notice.

Remember to use just enough energy to sustain mindfulness.

Probably what you noticed when your hands were lightly touching was that it takes very little energy to be aware. When I ask the question after doing this exercise on retreat the usual response is 'very little' and often 'none at all'. When we're not asking that the mind stick continuously to the sensations but just notice what's happening when you're aware, all that is needed is to be present to the object. Over time we build up continuity through reminding ourselves to be aware, but it's important we have the right sort of effort or attentiveness to start with.

If you've ever juggled you probably know it helps to be relaxed. You try to stay grounded and with your feet mostly in one place but able to take small steps when necessary to keep your centre of gravity under the juggling sacks. Your shoulders need to be relaxed and not tensed up around your ears.

One of the easiest mistakes in juggling is when you try and reach up to grab the falling sack out of the air rather than let it descend with gravity to drop into your hand. When you reach out and grab you use a lot of effort, which means there is less energy to simply notice what's happening and make subtle adjustments through the body. The wilder the movement towards the sack, the more time it takes to recover a neutral balanced stance, ready for the next falling juggling sack.

Being relaxed helps awareness and clear knowing to assess what needs to be done, both in juggling and in meditation, and to not do too much. It is natural to try to anticipate what's happening, but in doing so we are less receptive. We move towards the 'object' rather than allowing awareness with its broad perspective to take in what's happening and then do what is necessary. With practice, we can learn to let objects come to us, when mind and body is relaxed, spacious, and aware.

Not much energy is needed for awareness to grow. If you use too much effort you don't give mindfulness the conditions it needs to thrive. Effort and strong 'trying' can be like a great wind ruffling up the surface of an ocean, bringing high tides sweeping disruptively over land. It distorts the natural movement of the waves, and of the mind, bringing agitation and restlessness in its sway. What we are looking for is to observe things as they naturally occur, nothing more. It can be more helpful to think in terms of being mindful or being present, rather than 'trying' to be mindful.

Reducing unnecessary effort[3]

One way to think about the quality of effort used and to spot habitual ways of approaching any task is in terms of reducing any unnecessary effort. Just having this idea in the mind can prompt a new relationship to how we approach our meditation and our lives. We begin to more easily recognize 'trying hard' and 'I should' and 'I must' and similar mental and emotional motivators, and see the underlying views and attitudes that drive us.

Let's look further at persistence as applied to meditation particularly. *Ātāpī* has connotations of patience and not giving up. Because we are not using more energy than is necessary, awareness stays steady; it does not take a strenuous effort to be mindful. We need to have consistency and ease in the mind which allow mindfulness to be maintained throughout the day without becoming tired.

Sayadaw U Tejaniya is fond of saying that if you are tired at the end of a day of practice, you are using too much effort, which is tiring for the mind and creates tension in both body and mind. Meditation refreshes and balances the mind, so if we're practising well our energy should increase, not decrease. When we experience this, it can give us more confidence in our practice as we see the results of applying just enough energy.

I think this is a great way of assessing how we work in meditation: does the way I practise make me feel tired and depleted, or is awareness contributing to a sense of aliveness? What is the quality of the aware mind when we've practised with reducing any unnecessary effort? Of course, other factors such as a sleepless night can affect our energy and might increase the need for rest. Physical and emotional pain can also be very tiring, and it may take a long time before we have the skill in practice to be with all types of pain in such a way that it doesn't wear us down emotionally.

Continuity of awareness

Coming back to the line in the *Satipaṭṭhāna Sutta* that I quoted in chapter 1, it says we are mindful 'to the extent necessary for bare knowledge and continuous mindfulness'.[4] Our aim in being mindful is to have a continuity of moments where we're present and knowing what we're present to. More than this is extra and unnecessary. We might think that more effort is always better, but not in this case. We are not aiming for 'more' except in the sense of more *moments* when we're aware.

With more continuity and the right type of effort, awareness grows quite naturally to eventually become continuous. Through continuity of attention we begin to see more deeply how the mind functions, and enable awareness to make connections which lead, at first, to small insights and eventually to deep understandings. If we're only aware intermittently and sporadically, we won't be able to join the dots that lead to continuous knowing and deeper wisdom.

An important aspect of diligence, which doesn't really come out in the English word, is its association with the Sanskrit word *tapas*. It doesn't mean the tasty Spanish snacks, but heat or fire. Awareness is not a dry, cold observation of what is happening within, but a warm and sympathetic engagement with life. The qualities of interest and curiosity in the aware mind observing what's happening allow us to engage fruitfully with our experience, without getting so caught up in the drama of our stories.

Returning to the analogy of watching the mind like a naturalist, one figure who personifies such interest and curiosity, for me, is Sir David Attenborough. Anyone who has seen the documentaries he has been presenting on television for over fifty years will recognize his distinctive enthusiasm and sense of wonder for the natural world. However obscure or downright ugly the insect or minute sea creature is, he is warmly curious about it. Regardless of what he is investigating, his attitude is one of openness, delight, and deep engagement.

If we can bring even a small flavour of this attitude to our mindfulness practice, there will be enormous benefit. Any moments where we can recognize openness and interest in what we are observing will significantly change the experience. Without it, we will usually resort to force and subsequently build up emotional resistance and physical tension.

4. Free from Desires and Discontent (in Regard to the World of Sense Experience) (*Vineyya Abhijjhadomanassa*)

How does it feel to be content? Can you think of a time when you were content to be where you were and with whoever you were with? Cast your mind back to that time and see if you can reconnect with what it was like. It doesn't need to be an episode in your life where everything was going right and you had no problems or difficulties. It could be quite a fleeting experience that stands out in your mind because of the quality of it.

Perhaps it was a long summer afternoon riverside picnic with friends. Or you were up in the middle of the night rocking your sleepless baby and thinking there was nowhere else you'd want to be, not even asleep in your comfortable bed. Sometimes it might happen when you're meditating; your mind might feel as it often does with lots of thinking and plenty of moments of inattention and yet you're happy to be sitting there practising as best you can.

The chances are that you felt that everything was OK just as it was. There was no desire to make something else happen, or to prolong the experience and stretch out the pleasure of it. Perhaps there was a sense of timelessness in those moments even when the circumstances were quite ordinary and mundane.

This fourth factor of Right Mindfulness is a freedom from agitation in the mind, which leaves it deeply content. We might experience contentment when conditions in our lives are favourable – for example, when we're relaxing with friends – but this factor of mind, as with the story of the Buddha and King Bimbisāra, is more to do with the mind that accepts and is at ease with what is happening. It comes about through *not resisting* whatever is happening and this allows you to be fully present to the communication between you and your wide-awake infant at three o'clock in the morning. You can say 'this is what is happening in this moment'. There may be a 9am meeting coming up all too soon, but right now you are doing what needs to be done without struggle or wanting it to be otherwise.

The mind experiences contentment when we are largely free from the pushes and pulls of our 'desires and discontents'. Desires and discontent regarding 'the world' means the world of our physical senses. Often our choices and behaviours are led by our desire for certain sense experiences – the pleasant and enjoyable tastes, harmonious sounds, pleasing touches.

Equally, we'll often try to avoid other experiences such as a bad smell or a disturbing sight. Avoidance, while natural, disturbs the mind as we try to get away from what is actually happening. We experience desire and discontent through the mind sense too, such as when we desire the approval of others or criticize unnecessarily from a discontented state of mind. The feeling of discontent or dissatisfaction is often stimulated by not getting what we want. Both desire and discontent are agitating to the mind.

Contentment is the key to this fourth aspect of mindfulness. Through becoming more aware of our desires and discontented states of mind we are less caught up in them and identified with them. When the mind is less pushed and pulled about it is calmer and more contented. Contentment happens when the mind and heart are at ease.

The territory of 'desire' or craving is something that will come up again and again in this book. How can we relate to desire in a healthy way, one that is conducive to happiness rather than suffering?

Independence of mind

The implications of this lack of resistance to whatever happens to us, and the resulting ease and contentment, are profound. We become less dependent on external factors for our happiness, such as the baby sleeping when we want her to, or our work colleagues agreeing with our proposals, or our meditation going well. We find that our happiness is not dependent on something pleasant happening or continuing. Equally importantly, we can still access contentment without something unpleasant stopping or going away. Whatever is happening is simply an object to be known in our experience. It matters less if it is a pleasant (bird song) or unpleasant (pneumatic drill) 'object' but simply whether we can be aware of it.

A temporary but powerful freedom is born in the mind that is content. It is freedom from the suffering and frustration of trying to control things that are usually beyond our control. A good friend of mine likes to say, 'We have control over nothing, and influence over everything'. When we understand this, even for moments at a time, we cease struggling with what is happening. This doesn't mean we are passive and don't act when things are important to us. Instead we use the influence we do have. This might involve writing letters to our government, going on peaceful marches, or joining an organization that is working for a cause that is important to you.

Likewise, in our meditation practice we can't choose the results or a particular outcome, in that we can't *make* concentration or peaceful states arise. But we can influence the likelihood of reaching our goals by setting up the conditions we need to get there. When we are focused on an outcome, we often neglect factors *in the present moment* that are essential to reaching our goal. Another feature of focusing on where we are going rather than where we are is assuming we *know* where we're heading. This can close down more creative and *unknown* possibilities because we are not open to them.

Confidence in our practice

When we don't struggle with what is happening in our practice and our lives, we gain more confidence in what we can cope with. When we sit with physical pain, or depressed feelings, or the desire to get up and end the meditation, and feel some degree of acceptance of those things, we see that we can bear with them. We don't have to follow the urge to move away from pain, or to compound depression by adding strong judgements of ourselves. We start to come into a new relationship with 'objects' of experience where we can allow them to be there and lessen the compulsion to push away unpleasant things and hang on to pleasant enjoyable ones.

Confidence comes from seeing that it really is possible for anything to be an object in awareness. Dullness, sleepiness, or tension, as well as blissful states, can all simply be known and felt, but we know them from the perspective of the mind that is aware and at ease with what it is knowing. In this context, we can see that contentment is akin to equanimity, the balanced mind of wisdom.

Conclusion

These are the four aspects of 'Right Mindfulness' as the Buddha taught them:

Mindful
Clearly comprehending or clearly knowing
Diligent
Free from desires and discontent (in regard
      to the world of sense experience)

Together, these aspects help to remind us of how the mind feels when mindfulness is working well. They are not a check list to tick off but qualities you can notice in the mind that is relaxed and aware. You can aid that process by reminding yourself of the four aspects occasionally in your meditation and helping them lodge in the back of the mind. In this way, they start to become the natural perspective from which awareness views all experience. I will say more about this in chapter 4 on Right View and the wisdom perspective.

    You might like to find your own shorthand for these qualities or use the ones I offered at the beginning of this chapter, which are:

Present and receptive
Clearly knowing
Curious
Contented

You can remind yourself to check the quality of awareness regularly, and what you notice may alert you that something is missing. For example, you might become aware that you're not very interested in the practice (the right quality of effort is missing) or your thoughts are continually in the future (therefore directing the mind to present moment awareness would be helpful). Reminding yourself to notice what's happening can often be enough to stimulate the mind to remember the information you already have about how to work with the four factors.

In this way, we let awareness be simple and relaxed in the present moment. We let the mind and body be receptive to what is occurring, and notice natural curiosity when it is present. And when there is ease and contentment in the mind and heart, we are aware of that too.

Mindful Pause: Working with the Four Factors of Right Mindfulness

This exercise continues from the Touching Hands one in which we worked with the quality of effort used to support awareness. Here I'm going to bring in the other three qualities we've been looking at in this chapter.

While you carry on reading, just gently notice what you're aware of.

You may find that more things come into your awareness just through being asked to notice what you're aware of.

Or you may find that your awareness moves from one thing to another: for example, you notice the words on the page or screen, then you notice something physical, perhaps that you've just changed your posture and in retrospect you're aware of a twinge from a sore shoulder, then you notice your breath moving your rib cage in and out.

Just sit now, without reading, for a couple of minutes, perhaps with your eyes closed, but you can leave them open if you prefer. Don't try and direct your mind to do anything. Just sit and see what you notice.

Every now and again gently drop in the question 'am I aware?' or 'am I present?' Notice how the questions take you right into an awareness of the present moment.

You might be aware of any experience through your physical senses; what you're smelling or seeing or touching or hearing.

You can occasionally drop in a question to stimulate a spacious and attentive awareness. What's needed now? What is necessary for awareness?

Whether you're more aware of the objective world through your senses, or your own subjective 'knowing of experience', it doesn't matter; either is fine.

Are there moments where you notice interest or curiosity in the mind that's aware?

And you might recognize any moments of contentment and ease and feel what they're like in the mind and body.

Mindful Life Moment: 'Just let go and go where no mind goes. . .'[5]

You may well recognize the words above, courtesy of Khenpo Tsultrim Gyamtso Rinpoche. Maybe you've even sung them on retreat. During my time in Myanmar they have come to mind as I've meditated and reflected on awareness, on the mind, and above all practising staying present to experience.

Whatever that experience might be – for me, this morning, it was swimming in the Bay of Bengal, off the western coast of Myanmar, the sky a stunning blue, the sea a turquoise shimmer, the body weightless, and the mind in bliss. Two hours later, anxiety was creeping in as I walked up the beach looking for the village I'd set out for. Had I gone too far up the coast? (almost certainly). Was I getting sunburnt/dehydrated/knackered/bad-tempered? (yes to all of those).

Blissful, irritated, tired, hot, and sweaty. We can be aware of all these things and many more. And the quality with which we are aware can transform the experience. Awareness doesn't depend on a certain object to function. The balance, clear-sightedness, and impartiality of awareness allow pleasant or unpleasant experiences to be fully known. It is possible to be aware of anything that we can know through the physical senses and the same goes for the mind. Thoughts, feelings and other more subtle qualities in the mind can all be known.

Usually we're either focused externally – and I could feel that pull on the beach this morning towards beauty and the pleasure of the senses – or caught up in an internal dialogue – as with the thoughts and feelings fuelling anxiety when I was lost and overheating. Awareness allows both those processes to be known and, with practice, not identified with as 'me', 'my thoughts', etc. It does this through looking more internally at what is going on, through the wisdom aspect of Right Mindfulness – clearly knowing or comprehending and manifesting as a strong interest and a wise perspective.

We get interested in what is actually happening and distinguish that from our ideas and concepts about experience. Have you ever asked yourself: what is awareness? How do I know I'm aware? Does it make a difference to understand anxiety or irritation or sadness as a feeling in the mind and body?

I'm not asking these questions to try and answer them on a conceptual level but to let them point to the direct experience in that moment. Receptivity is needed for awareness to reveal what it is aware of and to just let things happen.

And sometimes that letting go allows us to know the mind in a new way, going where it's not gone before, to be completely present to the mysterious nature of awareness.

Chapter three

Watching Good TV
What We Are Aware Of

> When I was a young monk just starting to practice, I'd sit
> in meditation and sounds would disturb me. I'd think to
> myself, what can I do to make the mind peaceful? I took
> some beeswax and stuffed my ears with it. I couldn't
> hear anything. All that remained was a humming
> sound. I thought that would be peaceful, but no! All that
> thinking and confusion didn't arise at the ears after all, it
> was in the mind. That's the place to search for peace.[1]

In the *Satipaṭṭhāna Sutta*, the Buddha discusses what we can be aware
of. He divides a whole world of experience into just a few categories.
This is what I'll be exploring in this chapter. It is important to
remember, from the start, that *what* we're aware of is not as important
as *how* we are aware. When we are mindful with the qualities of
presence, interest, and contentment, *whatever* we're aware of will help
the mind develop in a positive way. Our primary interest is always the
knowing or the awareness rather than the objects of awareness. Even
though the object, the 'what' we are mindful of, is always secondary
to the quality of the awareness, the contents of experience are not
unimportant. We want to know how the mind works, so we need to
recognize the mental processes involved by watching the mind with
awareness. Despite the secondary importance of what we're aware
of there are many important things that can be learned from looking
at the 'object' side of experience.

In the *Satipaṭṭhāna Sutta*, the Buddha characterizes those 'objects'
into broad categories: body, feelings, mind, and *dhammas* (phenomena).

Leaving aside *dhammas* for now, let's look at the other three categories of experience, taking our own experience as the starting point.

Take a Few Moments to Notice What You're Aware Of

What is usually most immediate to awareness is the **body**. As you sit now you might notice the touch of clothing on your skin or the contraction or relaxation of muscles from holding the book in your hands or reaching out to pick up a mug of tea. You become aware of sensations that arise from breathing or sitting. As you notice further, you might become aware your neck muscles are a bit stiff from sitting still for a while, or that you can feel the touch of air on exposed skin on your hands. No doubt there will be many other tactile sensations depending on how long you pay attention. Some will be pleasant and others not.

There will be many other areas of our experience that come through all our senses that initially we might not notice. We *hear* the wind outside the window or become aware of the *smell* from a vase of flowers near us. Our physical senses pick up a wide range of experiences through what we see and taste, as well as touch, hear, and smell. We instinctively rely on our senses to help us navigate our way through the world and yet most of the time this process of sensing and processing experiences is completely unconscious and automatic. We are half aware of what is happening, taking in information at a subliminal level. When practising mindfulness, we are more consciously present to whatever we notice.

Moving on from the physical senses, you may also notice mental activity through the **mind**; thoughts, memories, and mental images come and go. There are many mental processes that go on without us being aware of them. We are perceiving, deciding, evaluating, and so on, all through the day. Mind is what enables us to be aware.

You may find you automatically *feel* something about the mental activity or whatever is experienced through the physical senses such as touch or sight. The **feeling tone** is not emotion, which is more complex with many mental factors acting together, but something subtle that happens as part of every moment we're conscious of something. Generally, by the time you've noticed 'feeling' there is already an added layer of interpretation that means we find any given experience either pleasant, unpleasant, or neutral in tone. There is a lot of interaction between the body, mind, and feeling tone as well as *reaction*.

Part of our work in meditation is to become aware of these different aspects of experience – body, feeling tone, and mind. I'll go into each of them in more detail below. Even though I will present them separately, in my experience there is a huge amount of overlap. A human being is an amazing thing, with all the complexities of our physical bodies, the capacities of our senses, and our sensitivities to emotional and mental nuance. What is even more amazing is how skilfully and automatically they all work together in an intricate dance, continually moving from the present moment to a subtly different new moment.

Body/Form (*Kāya*)

This is the first of the four satipaṭṭhānas and includes all the physical senses we experience through having a body. It is important not to over-identify this realm of experience just with the tactile body and touch sensations. Through the body we can see sights, hear all sorts of sounds, and smell and taste, as well as feel the sensations within the physical body.

Our experience becomes more fluid and vivid when we're aware of the interactive dance between the different senses, such as when we listen to music. We are hearing music, but we may also be moving the body as we tap our feet or nod in time to the beat. Another example of where senses come together, this time in quite a contrasting way, is found in the semi-tropics of Southeast Asia. If you've ever managed to eat the foul-smelling durian fruit, the smell of which is likened to old socks, sulphurous eggs, and cooked cabbage simultaneously, you'll find it quite pleasant. Most people, however, can't get beyond the smell, which has overwhelmed the sense of taste in this instance.

Even though our senses are at times seen to be quite distinct, as with the durian fruit, we tend to experience them through the overall context of the body – 'my' body which we mainly identify through the lens of tactile sensations. And so, this is where we'll start.

The relationship to our bodies is often complex. We're rarely content with the body we have. We want it to look a certain way – whether that be smaller in some areas, larger in others, more muscular in parts and pert in others, or softer or firmer in some way. Or we're unhappy when the body hurts and we worry about what will happen if it doesn't get better. We do things that we know aren't good for our bodies, like overeat and drink, or eat the wrong type of things; we ingest drugs – legal or not – or lie in the sun or a tanning shop for too long. We sit hunched over a desk and computer for many hours a day, ignoring the aches and tensions of the body from our sedentary habits. There are so many ways we live that deny the needs, and the realities, of our bodies.

This habitual denial can make the whole notion of 'body awareness' seem quite counter-intuitive. Why pay attention to something full of unpleasant sensations or that is a source of vague anxiety and dissatisfaction? It's no wonder that we seek distance by retreating to thoughts about our bodies or strategies to manage and control them in various ways. Or alternatively, how we can 'treat' and indulge them, or lastly, ignore them, lost in a world of the thinking mind.

James Joyce summed up the relationship some of us can have to our bodies with his character the awkward Mr Duffy, who 'lived a little distance from his body'.[2] He was not comfortable or at ease with his physicality, not even seeing it as part of him.

With mindfulness, we inhabit our bodies more fully through a warm and interested responsiveness.

Being with body sensations is simple, but our ideas and views about our physical body are often more compelling, and the sensations themselves are easily overlooked. What we think about our body, for example, and the actual direct experience of this living, breathing, sensing thing can be very different. Both modes of experience are important, but in meditation we want to move from predominantly being aware of the concepts and ideas we're using to label our experience, into actual physical experience.

It's not that one is wrong and the other right, but generally we have an overemphasis on the thoughts, images, and concepts *about* any experience. We're more familiar with a slightly removed or second-hand version where our ideas strongly influence the physical experience. For instance, it is almost hard-wired into our mental make-up that we should try and avoid any discomfort in the body. This view (which is not rationally thought out) can affect the amount of pain relief we take, or lead to distracting ourselves through such things as comfort eating or excessive TV, or simply to our minds being taken over by worrying about what's happening, all of which affect our overall health.

When we become aware of this idea that compels us to avoid even minimal pain, we make it more conscious, and perhaps see that it's unreasonable to think we'll go through our lives without any discomfort. Thinking in a helpful way about our experiences creates new possibilities and a spaciousness that allows us to relax away from the habitual circularity of our thoughts and views. What greatly supports being open to pain and discomfort, without resistance to it, or needing distraction from it, is learning to stay with the actual experience. Awareness becomes a doorway into another mode of perceiving.

We can discover that there is a whole universe of tactile experience once we open to it: a world of temperature, pressure, softness, firmness, tension, relaxation, vibration, and movement. When we are more attuned to our experience and can know it directly, we are able to notice how even these qualities are not static, and nor is it possible to completely separate them out in this way. There is simply a flow of experience that we can call sensation.

World of Sensing

We usually take our senses for granted – unless, that is, we have partially or completely lost the use of one of them. They are a completely natural part of who we are, who I am. Looking at our experience of the five physical senses, we start to see them in a different light and perhaps begin to question some assumptions about ourselves.

Initially when we're mindful we become more aware of *what* we're sensing – the sights and sounds, the tastes, smells, and tactile worlds. We notice specific 'objects' of sight when watching the TV or crossing a busy road. If we are present to some degree, we'll hear the traffic sounds or a nearby dog barking, and we'll notice the saltiness of the soup we're tasting. We'll breathe in the crispness of the air on a bright wintry day and feel the coldness on our face.

When we're present to ourselves and our world, we experience life more vividly through our senses. We can feel more alive, awake, and joyful. We 'stop and smell the roses'! We spend less time caught up in thoughts and complicated stories about the past or fantasizing about the future. We really are 'there', whether that is washing up or preparing for our Dharma class, rather than rattling through the activity to have a bit of time 'off duty'. We see that it makes a difference to how we feel when we're more aware, and often others notice the changes too.

However, this is just the first step in the journey of mindfulness.

We're looking to become aware of our own body and mind and investigate the inner experience that is usually implicit and therefore taken for granted. In order to use mindfulness to investigate, we need to come close to the source of our experiences. The next step, while not denying *what* we're seeing or smelling, is to *know*, or be aware, that 'seeing' or 'smelling' are happening. We rest more attention with what's actually happening, and what is happening is that our senses are registering information. We have taken a step further back from external 'objects' and become aware of the process closer to the source. 'Seeing' is knowing sights, the sense of touch is aware of tactile sensations, 'hearing' is knowing sounds. We bring awareness to the sense itself, rather than what is being sensed, which we can call the sense object. We apply this across the board to tasting, touching, smelling, hearing, and seeing and through this awareness we can know the experience more directly.

As we become more aware, we can notice that, much of the time, sense activity is going on outside of our awareness. Our eyes are open most of the time except when we're sleeping or meditating, but we're not usually aware that we're seeing. This is one of the reasons it can be so helpful to meditate with your eyes open, at least from time to time. If we always meditate with closed eyes, we don't get the chance to practise 'seeing' in helpful conditions away from the overload of stimuli which can change, at great speed, in our day-to-day lives.

Occasionally we get the opportunity to examine how our senses work when we temporarily lose one. We can come to see how much the sense is simply going about its own business of 'sensing' without impinging on our awareness at all.

A few years ago, I had a sore throat and decided I would take a herbal remedy which had been popular with Westerners during my stays in Myanmar. It had been a while since I'd taken it and I was in a hurry, so rather than checking the instructions for use, I simply squirted a few drops towards the back of my throat.

A few things happened in quick succession: I missed my throat and the drops landed on the back of my tongue. It tasted disgusting, really bitter, and burned slightly. I then had a memory of how the drops should be administered – which was by gargling a cup of warm water with a few drops mixed into it!

The result was that my tongue felt quite numb and the bitter taste lasted a few hours. What I didn't realize until my next meal was that it was to be the last thing I tasted for a while. I'd managed to burn most of the taste buds on my tongue, and initially (in those pre-Google days) I didn't know if they would regrow or not!

This gave me the opportunity to explore taste, ironically through a lack of ability to taste, and also touch sensations. What is left when taste is not there? Well, it is mainly texture, which I discovered is not quite enough when it comes to being motivated to eat. Texture was mainly about lumps of different sizes and consistencies and was not very appealing. Each time I ate felt as if I was chewing wet cardboard.

I realized how much the role of taste influenced what I ate, and how much I ate. Without taste, there was virtually no pleasure in food, and therefore little desire to eat. I could understand from this experience how difficult it was for patients being treated for some cancers who lose their sense of taste and are in danger of suffering from malnutrition. In the few days before those precious little buds grew back, I had a keener sense of the relationship between tasting and enjoyment, and how if we don't enjoy something, or get some pleasure from it, the mind simply says 'why bother?'

When pleasure isn't a factor, eating becomes much more about nutrition and managing energy. The question becomes 'what do I need to eat?' rather than 'what do I want to eat?' From a practice standpoint, we can see more clearly the role of craving in the process of eating and how much the pursuit of pleasure drives our behaviour. There is nothing wrong with pleasure, of course, but if it weighs too heavily as a factor in our decisions, we will overeat.

And as a general factor of mind, if we consistently choose pleasure over awareness, as we will see in a later chapter, craving will grow, and awareness will not. We are always growing habits in the mind through our thoughts, our speech, and our actions. When we seek to gratify our senses, we may initially be able to do so while remaining aware, but eventually awareness will weaken. The Buddha reminded his disciples constantly that what we feed grows, so it is our choice in every moment: do we want to feed craving or feed awareness?

Awareness encourages us to 'stay with' what is happening. We do this through becoming familiar with a subtle and always present mental factor which can be known in experience. This is what the Buddha called 'hedonic tone' or 'feeling tone' and is what we will explore next.

Feeling Tone (*Vedanā*)

The Buddha listed 'feeling' as one of the four satipaṭṭhānas, the spheres of experience that we can know. Often talked about as 'feeling tone' or 'hedonic tone', there are plenty of interpretations for the Pali term *vedanā*. One area of confusion is that we commonly use words describing feeling and emotion interchangeably, but emotion comes about through a complex mix of thoughts, images, memories, and physical sensations in the body. Our pulse might increase, or we start to sweat, or we can't think straight; all these things are manifestations of emotion, and there are many, many more. We could say that feeling tone is the springboard from which emotion kicks off, but, independently of emotion, it is a subtle aspect of experience that is tricky to describe.

Feeling tone is not emotion, whether difficult and painful emotions or joy-filled emotional states. We might use the language of feeling to say, 'I feel very sad' (using the words to express an emotion) or 'I feel like a pizza tonight' (where we are expressing a preference or desire.) These examples are not what the Buddha meant when he was talking about the hedonic or feeling tone.

Neither is it the physical sensations that we 'feel' when we say, for example, 'My leg feels really sore from when I fell over.'

In every moment of experience there will be a variety of feeling tones happening quite automatically. We don't have to do anything to make them happen and we can't stop them through using our will. For us to be able to see or hear or use any of our physical senses, three things need to come together. We need to have a working sense 'door' – for example, the faculty of hearing. This comes together with a sense object (a sound), and the third essential component is a mind that is conscious or knowing. In each moment there are many different sense 'contacts' coming together between the mind, the sense door, and the sense object.

Feeling Tone Is Conditioned

The hedonic or feeling tone arises from a collaboration of conditions coming together. In every moment of experience there will be a variety of feeling tones happening quite automatically. Some will be pleasant, others unpleasant, and a great many will be quite neutral and go largely unnoticed. We don't have to do anything to make feelings happen and we can't stop them through using our will. The feeling tone happens very fast and is not discernible to the everyday mind, but with practice we can rest more with the feeling in any given experience and notice for ourselves how that moment is experienced.

You can tune into the feeling tone in any moment. You could try now, just settling into awareness of sensations in the body wherever awareness lands. In my own case, I can feel tingling and warmth in my hands, and the point of contact between the hardness of computer keys and my fingertips. What I've described are the sensations from that contact, but what can also be known is how the mind *feels* in relation to those sensations. This is not something I make happen but something I can notice; the warmth of my hands feels pleasant, the touch on the keyboard feels more neutral.

When the working sense door, the sense object, and consciousness come together (in the case of 'seeing', a fourth factor is necessary which is light), there will be some sort of feeling tone. To give you an example, when the mind is consciously knowing, the eyes are working, and the computer screen is seen some sort of feeling tone will arise. This feeling tone will be conditioned by how we've responded to this object in the past. If we've liked it, it will feel pleasant and if we've disliked or rejected the object in the past, we will be conditioning an unpleasant feeling response. A third option is that sometimes, as is the case when looking at my computer screen, it may feel quite neutral. In every moment of experience there will be a feeling tone that appears in one of these three ways.

Vedanā, feeling tone, is conditioned by our historical experiences and these responses to stimuli can build up over time. I have a cute photo of me at about eighteen months old with a large ice cream cone, and sticky sweet stuff all over my face and running down towards my elbow. I learned to like ice cream early in life and that has continued (so far) well into my middle years. But this response from past conditions is not absolute. It is affected by conditions in the present moment. If I have a sore tooth, ice cream might be the last thing I want, or if I'm chilled, I'd probably prefer a hot drink to warm me up. The feeling tone can also be influenced by changes in our physical make-up such as hormones, which might cause us to grow out of a sweet tooth and start preferring savoury foods.

If we can be aware of how our responses to things change it can help us be less attached to getting what we want because it's pleasant and rejecting what we don't want because we view it as unpleasant. Usually we think the feeling tone is *within the thing itself* – rather than a conditioned response that happens in our own mind. We perceive that sadness and a sore leg are unpleasant and that pizza is very pleasant. Actually, the feeling tone arises from the contact, the connection when those three things come together, and is not integral to just one of them (i.e. the sense object).

If the hedonic tone was *within* the pizza, we would always find it pleasurable, the very nature of pizza would be pleasant. But sometimes we get a bland one, or it arrived too cool at the table, or we're not feeling very well and just the thought of pizza makes us nauseous. Even if every one we ate was delicious, however much we love pizza, if we had to eat one every day for a week, we'd probably get a craving for something else!

Mindful Pause: Using Awareness to Investigate Feeling Tone

You can be sitting, walking, or lying down to do this exercise, or even standing, as long as you can be quiet. Settle into the moments of movement and stillness, of sound and sights. Rest inside yourself in a relaxed and open way.

Tune into how you (the mind) feels. You don't need to label this as an emotion, or even know whether the feeling is pleasant or unpleasant. Simply know that the mind is feeling. It's a natural function of the mind, it's part of the mind, *and* part of what the mind is knowing.

Here are some areas of investigation and exploration in relation to feeling. Don't try to find answers, but simply let the mind play with the question.

> How does feeling differ from knowing sensation?
> Do you tend to 'locate' feeling into a part of the body?
> How do you know feeling is happening?
> Can you recognize the feeling of present moment awareness?

Feeling can be a very helpful anchoring object, so you can use it as you might use the breath while you're going about your daily life. Just check in every now and again or keep centred by knowing feeling.

At other times, you might do this exercise to identify different feelings, and whether they are pleasant or unpleasant or more neutral feelings in your experience.

Our Ideas Affect How We Feel About Things

Vedanā is affected by our thoughts and ideas about what we experience. When we meditate, we can have unconscious ideas about what should be happening. When the experience that is happening outside our meditation hall is, let's say, bird song, we experience it not just as pleasant, but 'right'. We have the unconscious idea that that sound of birds singing belongs there!

When the local air force base sends fighter jets roaring over our retreat centre for the whole meditation, we can find ourselves disturbed and annoyed and even think we can't meditate under those conditions. Often, we fail to recognize the ideas in the mind that say, 'this does not belong here, it should not be happening whilst I'm meditating!' All we have to go on is that we find the experience thoroughly unpleasant.

Actually, both the bird song and the fighter jets are simply sounds, and part of the sense of 'hearing'. But because of different ideas in the mind we relate to one as pleasing and the other as displeasing. Those ideas and views might be about armed forces and wars or simply the conditions we think are necessary for meditation; either way, they are just that – ideas, conceptions about our experience, rather than the experience itself, which is 'hearing' happening.

Feeling tone interacts in each moment with another mental quality that's always arising with momentary experience. This is *perception* or recognition. It is perception that recognizes an experience we've had before and remembers it through storing it in a growing perceptual database. This means we can take mental short cuts and don't have to mentally reconstruct a sight (this is a table) or a sound (a knock on the door) or a taste from scratch each time. We label our world through repetition over time.

As babies, early on we start to recognize the face, smell, and sound of our parents or other significant caregivers. At around the age of one year old, we can vocalize names for those precious 'objects' – 'mama', and so on. Over our lives we continue to add labels to objects, including naming subtle mental processes such as thinking, remembering, fantasizing, or complex planning, until the data bank is huge, and many objects from any of the senses can be instantly recognized.

Along with recognition comes a feeling tone. 'Mama' is associated with pleasant feelings at times when she feeds and cuddles us. At nappy change or when we're left to cry or talked to in a rough way, those feelings will be experienced as unpleasant. In the same way, a memory bank of perceptions builds up; pleasant, unpleasant, and neutral associations are also conditioned over time and repeated happenings. Feeling and perception are both subtle mental events that arise very close together in the mind. However, their *nature* is different. It sounds obvious, but the role of feeling is to feel, and the job of perception is to perceive and to interpret what is perceived. I hope the example below helps you get a sense of how they work together.

On retreat in Myanmar a friend described a small incident. She had been watching her mind in the close but relaxed and light way emphasized by U Tejaniya and noticed some slight tickling sensations on her neck. She didn't know what was causing the sensations but watched her mind go between two different possibilities. She wasn't consciously thinking about what was tickling her neck, rather she was noticing what the mind was doing quite automatically.

First, there was an image/thought of a mosquito and she noticed a corresponding feeling tone that was unpleasant with a slight shrinking back from the experience. This was followed by the mind finding another possibility: her hair was being lifted by the gentle movement of the ceiling fan and brushing across her skin. This was accompanied by a mildly pleasant feeling. She watched the mind go back and forth – mosquito or hair? – and the feeling tone that automatically accompanied each one. It was clear that 'mosquito/unpleasant' was conditioned by previous mosquito bites and subsequent itchiness as well as ideas that mosquito bites were 'bad', even dangerous, and to be avoided. These ideas fed back into the experience that the feeling was unpleasant.

The idea of hair brushing against skin may have very different associations to do with femininity and attractiveness – we don't know in this case – but the main point is that the experience itself was pleasant.

So here it is very clear that depending on the ideas in the mind we will experience different feeling tones. The more aware we are of our experience, the more we'll notice things about the mind that are usually hidden to us. They are hidden through inattention and lack of awareness, or from relating more to concepts and ideas than to our direct experience. With awareness, we're able to access an inner world that changes radically how we relate to feelings and perception.

Awareness enables us to make choices based on the 'live' present moment situation, rather than a potentially outdated and incorrect one based on conditioned historical or biased responses. With the example above, my friend was aware and curious and therefore not driven by the unpleasant feeling which probably would have meant shaking off the potential mosquito and avoiding a bite. On the surface that sounds like a good idea, but then she would have missed an opportunity to learn something about how the mind was working. Recognizing feeling and perception 'in action' takes both mindfulness and wisdom working to see what is happening.

By *staying with* the experience rather than acting habitually she also saw she didn't need to react hastily. Some of the ideas in her mind were conditioned through wanting to avoid discomfort. Others were just not true or accurate, such as the fear of the mosquito carrying malaria or dengue fever. With mindfulness she was able to recollect that the conditions – the location and time of year – were not right. The mosquito bite would have stung for a few minutes but was otherwise harmless.

I appreciate this is quite counter-intuitive for most of us. There are things we do (swipe at the mosquito) or don't do because of our ethical practice, our cultural conditioning, and the views and ideas designed to protect 'me'. Of course, our self-protective instincts serve an important function in times of danger, such as avoiding eating poisonous foods, but all too often this 'danger' warning is switched on to avoid *anything* unpleasant. The result is that we act with aversion and avoidance of the feeling rather than staying with awareness.

There are many implications if we are able to 'stay with the feeling' or the actual experience, rather than reacting in an automatic way full of assumptions and generalizations. Our communication becomes healthier when we can listen to what another person is saying and not have it filtered through our own reactions. And we become less dependent on our almost instinctual bias towards seeking out the pleasant and avoiding what we find unpleasant. We can therefore make value-driven choices rather than pleasure-seeking ones.

When we act on an unpleasant feeling, we may give vent to small or large acts of irritation, or even hatred, that we'll later regret. Whether it's killing a mosquito or shouting at our child or gossiping about a work colleague, it doesn't usually feel good afterwards. Acting on a pleasant feeling can also lead to suffering – overeating and drinking, staying up too late when we have an early start next morning. Having an awareness of what's driving us helps us make wiser choices.

Mind (*Citta*)

Mind (*citta* in Pali), body, and feelings are not separate but interrelate and interact in every moment. Later in the book we'll go into this relationship more – in fact, quite a lot of the book bumps up against this very thing, over and over again. For now, let's look at what is meant by 'mind'.

Mind in Buddhism is a broad concept. It includes all our internal experience of thoughts, mental images, our moods and perceptions, the volitions which drive our actions, and it includes the capacity for awareness, or mindfulness.

In the West, 'mind' is often contrasted with 'body', and with 'head and heart'. Especially in Dharma circles, we can tend to be a little dismissive of 'mind' as rational, cool, and heady, and see the body more positively as grounded and full of its own wisdom. The heart, too, is given more weight and importance as the emotional centre of our lives which we ignore at our peril. These views are natural and understandable given our tendency in the West to overvalue the intellectual world of rational thought and dry ideas. It makes a lot of sense that we re-emphasize a need to connect with our physical nature and ground in tactile sensations.

It is worth remembering, though, that the head/heart or mind/ body split that is so familiar to us is not part of the Eastern lexicon –

not in the Buddha's day, and not now in modern-day India, Myanmar, and many other countries where Buddhism is practised in Asia. The word *citta* has broader associations than our typical understanding of 'mind'. It is not a cold logic that can be separated from either the physical senses or the 'feel' of the mind. *Citta* is often translated as 'mind-heart' to give some indication that it is a broad term covering much ground.

However it is translated, there is no getting away from the mystery of the mind. We're not talking about the brain here, but of how we think or cognize or be conscious of something. The brain has a shape and a location in the head, though we must take that on faith to some degree, as we can't see it ourselves. The mind, without colour, texture, or form, is even less tangible and more elusive.

Knowing the Mind

One thing you might notice when you meditate is that you can't tell where thoughts are happening. We tend to say they happen in the head or the mind, but we don't know anything about the inside of our head directly. We only know we have a head because of a whole lot of ideas and memories that we put together. Awareness is not in the head, rather the head is an idea that is in awareness. In fact, we have no idea where awareness is.[3]

Although the mind has no physical form which we can touch, and we can't recognize it through its colour or shape like other objects, we can 'know' and 'feel' the mind through its functions and capacities, and its ability to recognize 'objects' of experience through the five physical senses. We use our capacity for self-awareness– a self-reflexive 'knowing that we know' – to be aware of the mind, our sixth sense. This gives us the ability to be aware of our thoughts and emotions, and to know or discriminate between different types of thoughts such as memories or planning thoughts.

Awareness enables us to be aware of both body and mind and is itself an aspect of mind. Whilst we all have some degree of reflexive awareness, we don't tend to cultivate that awareness, or see the tremendous benefits of doing so. To the extent that we learn to watch our minds we are less driven by our mental and emotional habits and able to be in the driving seat itself. Taking the metaphor further, when we're driving, we can see what's around us, see the road ahead, and make positive choices about the direction we're going in.

Mind and Object

When we talk about 'knowing the mind', this is not just knowing the different mental functions. When we watch the mind, we can recognize experiences arising from any of the five physical senses as well as from the mind. We are aware of all 'objects' through the mind sense, whether that be particular body sensations or our emotions. For this reason, it's important the quality of awareness is relaxed and broad; when the attention is focused on the objects of experience – the individual sights, sounds, or smells, for instance – we don't necessarily see what is happening in the mind. For watching the mind to happen, we need to settle back into a more open and spacious relationship to objects rather than the strong involvement of focusing, and notice how the mind is working.

Another way of talking about the 'how' and 'what' we're aware of is through a shift in perspective when we watch the mind. This comes about when we pay less attention to the *contents* of experience and become more interested in the *process* of how the mind is working.

Imagine a camera lens that is pointing outwards. It takes in all that is before it, whether that be a scenic view or a cityscape or a family portrait. This is the content or *object* side of the equation. Now imagine taking a mental step back to the person behind the camera, taking the picture. There will be several mental processes going on: the photographer is seeing and probably thinking, assessing, and deciding when to take the photo. No doubt there will be feeling tones associated with what is being seen and perhaps connected with the anticipation of taking a good picture. This is the *mind* side of the equation.

Often these mental processes of feeling, thinking, and assessing remain largely unnoticed so that we act quite unconsciously, and the thoughts and feelings happen outside of awareness. When watching the mind, we get to know these mental processes and the physical ones which will follow on from mental activity. We can observe, for example, seeing a near miss between a pedestrian and a car, and feel the reaction of contraction in the body, and shock in the mind. In mindfulness and wisdom practice we want to understand the interrelationships – or processes – happening between the body and mind, and between objects and the mind that is aware of them.

Mental experiences such as thoughts and memories are also 'objects' even though they are part of the mind; in fact, anything that can be known by awareness is an object arising in experience.

When we are aware of mental and physical processes, we are still aware of content. When we are aware of a thought, we also naturally know what the thought is about. But when we are aware of a thought as just a thought arising in the mind, as a mental process, we are less taken in by the content of the thought. The same is true for each of the five physical senses, for example hearing: if we practise knowing a sound as sound, we will still know what the sound is, whether it's a car passing by or our friend calling to us.

Process and content and mind and object are two sides of the same coin and both will be present in each moment of experience. When awareness is stronger and more continuous it is possible to see clearly the distinct nature of both mind and object, and the awareness that knows both.

Watching the Mind

One of Sayadaw U Tejaniya's students once said that watching the mind was like watching good TV! The student found it fascinating to see, for example, how the mind made judgements, decided things with limited information, created storms of emotion from a single moment of seeing or hearing or thinking. Even on those occasions when the content seemed pretty ordinary – another breath, familiar sounds, endless thinking – he saw what a difference it made when he was aware.

When we are aware, rather than watching 'same old' content, actually we're immersed in the mystery of watching the mind. Of course, the content is never really familiar and known to us. When we're fresh to the moment we can appreciate that each moment is new, each breath has never been before and will never come again. We can see habits of mind or memories, but they are always arising from the particular set of conditions that come from this particular moment. The mind is a living, breathing, creating thing. Just like a good BBC drama!

Mindfulness of Having Fun!

Sometimes our unconscious views will affect how we feel about the content. We might exclude some moments or activities because we don't think we can be aware when we're talking or watching TV! So, we might decide it's not worth bothering to try and instead switch off during those times.

It is helpful to remind ourselves that watching the mind can happen in any moment and in any situation. One of my favourite memories from a recent retreat came not during the actual retreat but afterwards when several of the team were hanging out. We were in a train travelling up a mountain in the Bernese Oberland and everyone was relaxed and feeling happy. A friend and I got into improvising a little Swiss tune that had been sung by half the retreatants at the end of the retreat. Believe it or not, the song was about a little slug caught out by its own greed. We added our own extra words in English, riffed off each other singing, and shrieked with laughter, drawing a certain amount of attention within the carriage.

Previously I might have judged myself unaware in that moment because we were larking around and making quite a lot of noise and having so much fun! But I knew for myself that I was aware in those moments. I could feel it, it was undeniable. And this is tremendously freeing as it wipes out any ideas that mindfulness *has* to be practised in an environment that is quiet and peaceful, that *I* myself must be quiet and feel peaceful! It's a practice that works when I feel rowdy and slightly disruptive or when my mood is low and unmotivated. It is still just a question of noticing what is happening. I find this radical and wonderful in its simplicity and effectiveness.

Of course, for quite a bit of the preceding ten days we had been relatively quiet on retreat, and awareness was helped along by the supportive framework of the retreat. But we need our practice to be effective off the cushion and outside of specific conditions to really take it into our lives.

Body, feeling tone, and mind, these are the first three of the four satipaṭṭhānas, the different categories of experience that the Buddha draws our attention to in the *Satipaṭṭhāna Sutta*. These categories are quite comprehensive. The take home message is '*whatever* we experience we can be aware of it'. We might not always be able to name it or understand it, but we can always be aware of it.

But there is a fourth satipaṭṭhāna which adds to the wisdom dimension of the practice. It is to this aspect that we turn our attention in the next chapter.

Mindful Life Moment: Addiction to the Senses

Shortly before leaving Myanmar on my first visit, I left the retreat centre for a day to shop for gifts to take home. I took a taxi divested of any soft furnishings except the seat, and spent a very happy few hours with a friend traipsing around covered city markets and eating pizza for lunch, our first Western-style food in months.

When returning to the centre that evening, we bumped into U Tejaniya, and spilled out our abundance of retreat energy joy.

'Yangon is beautiful', I gushed.

Sayadaw had a good laugh at that one. 'It's not Yangon that is beautiful,' he said. 'It's your *mind*.'

Of course!

Yangon is a fascinating city, with stunning ancient stupas and colonial elegance sitting alongside each other. Street stalls with friendly and curious vendors sell heaps of colourful fabrics or exotic fruits. Yangon is also a city of broken paving stones, foul-smelling rubbish heaps decaying in the heat of the tropical sun, and mangy dogs with starving pups. Buildings are black from pollution and, when I look carefully, the poverty is visible in every glance.

Yes, Yangon is beautiful, but it is also ugly. How it is perceived depends on the quality of the mind perceiving and experiencing it, but we forget this. It takes constant reminders to bear this perspective in mind. We automatically reset to prioritizing the objects of experience, rather than the mind that is knowing all these sense experiences.

We land on objects as if they were a life buoy in the middle of the ocean, rather than with the lightest touch that allows us to rest with the mind. We think the sense objects are our salvation, that they will rescue us from all the dis-ease of our lives. Just another sunset, or fine wine, or step up the career ladder will sooth the angst of the moment. Another stroke, hug, or movie night will reassure us that the unsettledness and uncertainty we feel hovering on the edge of consciousness is just an illusion. Resting with sense objects, rather than the mind knowing them, allows us to keep the nature of our lives at bay.

To stay with awareness, with the knowing quality, is a kind of renunciation; it puts the grasping onto sights and sounds, tastes, touches, and smells into their rightful place within the play of experience.

Occasionally this addiction to the senses can be felt in awareness with the force of an insight, and when we feel it, we naturally want to rest with awareness. And from awareness, we see that the addiction we take to be normal, proper life is anything but.

Chapter four

A Dharma Perspective
How the Buddha Would Have Thought

> The more you consider your experience in the light of
> the doctrines and practices taught by the Buddha, the
> clearer a sense you will get of what freedom from the
> fetters might mean. This is what is called Right View.[1]
>
> Right View comes first, to deal with the defilements.
> Start with wisdom, start from the top down.[2]

Being aware means that each of the four aspects of Right Mindfulness,
which we looked at in chapter 2, are online to some degree. We are
aware in the present moment; there is a sense of purpose and clearly
knowing what is happening as well as some ease and contentment
in the mind. Finally, the quality of energy or effort is consistent and
not strained. Already within these four qualities are elements of the
wisdom mind, through clear knowing and the mind that is free from
desires and discontent and the hindrances these words stand for. We
are looking to prime the mind, not only to encourage awareness but
also to find a way of viewing our experience that encourages wisdom
and *vipassanā* – clear seeing. It is the wisdom aspect I want to give
more attention to in this chapter.

It is hard to overstate the importance of wisdom, or insight, in a life
of practice. Some metaphors used in the Buddha's teaching to express
the mind that has wisdom or understanding are 'crossing to the
further shore' and 'setting an upside-down pot upright'. The goal of
Awakening is simultaneously a journey to undertake and a radically
new perspective. Our study of Buddhism, while indispensable, can
only take us so far. Wisdom is not intellectual understanding or facts

that can be learned from a book, or increasingly from Google! Wisdom is a direct, intuitive understanding that, while aided and supported by the conceptual mind, goes way beyond it.

In my early days of practising I was involved in writing for the magazine published by my local Buddhist Centre. I conducted a series of interviews called 'Why We Are Friends' with members of our sangha. One of the articles I wrote featured two friends: a Buddhist psychotherapist and the Chair of the Buddhist Centre. They were extremely different characters and yet had been close friends for many years. Part of the attraction – and frustration – for the one who ran the Buddhist Centre was that his friend freely admitted to deep experiences he couldn't describe. Both men, in their own ways, were highly articulate but the psychotherapist stuck to his guns; it was not always possible to fully articulate some experiences. For his friend, this was fascinating and he learned to be open to experiences about which little could be expressed conceptually.

It is this type of experience that can emerge from awareness and eventually manifest as a clear seeing into the nature of reality. When we prioritize qualities of mind and heart we directly know and downgrade the importance of conceptually understanding our experience (*thinking about* things) through resting more with awareness, we've set up the conditions by which insights, large and small, can manifest.

In Buddhism, wisdom is contrasted with 'delusion' or 'ignorance'. Ignorance is likened to a monkey stuck in mud or quicksand. With every attempt to free himself by putting a hand or foot on the ground to lever himself out of the mud he becomes more and more embedded in his sticky tomb. Our human predicament is similarly mired in delusion; we are caught in a web of ideas and beliefs, and compelling and disturbing emotions prevent us understanding a way out of our struggles and suffering.

I recently saw a physiotherapist for a painful shoulder. I'd been doing two different sets of exercises, one set prescribed by my GP and the second series from a telephone consultation with a health professional. I did the exercises for a couple of months with no decrease in the swelling or pain. After examining me, the physiotherapist concluded that the exercises were probably overusing the collar bone, where she thought the real problem was. Her suggestion was to stop doing all the exercises and see what happened. This felt both revolutionary, and intuitively right, as it turned out to be.

Our first step out of delusion and towards wisdom is often to just become aware of what is actually happening. This can feel counter-intuitive because we are going against familiar habits of body, speech, and mind that want us to act – usually to further our own agenda or to get us out of a situation or emotional state. In our hurry to act we can mentally step over what's already happening and miss it altogether. To some degree, we still know what's happening – for example, we're distressed or agitated, or we're stressed from a lot of work – but we're usually very quickly in 'sort it out' mode rather than just being aware of what's happening, which can bring a more resourced mind state to a problem.

Intimacy with All Things?

Many years ago, I was in Spain in early spring during the period when the almond trees blossom. I remember one day being driven through the dry rocky landscape of the Spanish interior. I was watching my mind, content and aware of all the mind was taking in, with the visual sense feeling particularly alive. The pink frothy beauty of the blossom was everywhere, and sitting in the back of the car I was quietly ecstatic. Then a thought came: 'this is just pleasant experience'. With the thought was some separation from the delightful experience. My heart closed, just a little, and the joyful state diminished. At the time, I felt slightly regretful that seeing the experience more clearly lessened the feeling of happiness in the mind. In that moment, mindfulness and a dharma perspective seemed a bit of a spoilsport.

But is it really the case that being mindful also leads to less openness to beauty and delight, including the beauty of the natural world? Awareness is usually seen as a way of enabling this attitude, of notions of reverence for life and intimacy with experience, but I seemed, at least in that moment, to be experiencing the opposite. In our increasingly disjointed and automated lives we give high value to those moments of feeling intimate with life, as they feel so rare. Does awareness mean we're closing off to those times through looking to also see the experience more for what it is and through bringing some objectivity to what is happening in experience?

Sometimes the language of awareness and wisdom, and of 'objects' and 'observing' experience, can be a bit of a turn-off. In my teaching, I've seen that for some students the language to describe the process of watching the mind can feel cool or overly detached and this sets up resistance to being mindful. There's a feeling of constriction and tightness and an almost irresistible impulse to rebel! They don't want to just 'know' or 'see' or to stand back from things but to be involved. For most of us, we want to know where the juiciness of life is and plunge right in. After all, which sounds more attractive? Intimacy with life, or detachment from the objects of experience? Or could it be a false distinction? I'll come back to this towards the end of the chapter.

It is at least partly an issue of how the different strands of Buddhist history talk about practice. The Buddha's early teachings are full of negation. Enlightenment is described through what it is *not*. It's pared down and scraped back so that you can clearly see what's left. Terms like 'the void', 'the deathless', or 'the unborn' abound. And this makes sense when you're trying to avoid using concepts that suggest spiritual realization is a 'thing' existing somewhere or something to get hold of. Those traditions say it's easier and more accurate to say what Enlightenment or Awakening *is not*.

Later Buddhist teachings go to the other extreme, with lush flowery language and an impossible abundance of mythic and imaginative suggestiveness. The words and concepts are painting a picture and are not to be taken literally; they are the finger pointing at the moon, rather than the moon of Awakening itself. The focus is on the interconnectedness of all things, and the teachings augment rather than strip away. We are left with everything rather than nothing.

We come to the same realization but from complementary paths. For most people, both perspectives will be helpful at different stages of their spiritual journey. And 'nothing' and 'everything', in the end, are much the same thing.

Perhaps you can bear this in mind as we go through the chapter and notice how you are relating to the words I'm using, especially the language of 'objects'. If you become aware of some resistance – great! You're aware of it! How you work with the mind that resists will hopefully become clear.

We're Always Coming from a View

It is completely possible to hold views and most of the time not know it! A relatively small number of our views will be explicit and consciously held by us. An example of an explicitly held view would be when we vote in an election for the political party or candidate whose views most correspond to our own.

More frequent are the implicit views we hold. Often our friendships and relationships are formed because we share views without necessarily realizing it. We might notice a feeling of pleasure and 'rightness' and feel affirmed and secure when we're with certain people. We might say quite innocently, 'We've got so much in common', without quite realizing that our own views are being comfortingly reinforced each time we meet this person, or even think about them.

Often, we have no idea what our view or perspective is until we bump up against someone else's view that is different to our own. Living in various Buddhist residential communities as I have done over the years, I've seen this play out repeatedly. Whether it is the right way to wash up, or how clean the house is kept, or how carefully or carelessly someone treats our belongings, suddenly it all matters to us more than we ever would have thought. We can get quite upset when implicit views and values we hold are challenged or dismissed. Our internal narrative can be full of complaint in a way that living alone doesn't reveal. When we live or work closely with others, we can find ourselves thinking, 'Why don't others see this is the best way', or even the *only* way, or their way is annoying. All this is very fruitful to notice and useful in getting to know the habits of our minds.

As we saw in the previous chapter, our views, ideas, and opinions form over time and are affected by different sorts of conditioning in our lives. Education, family background, the number of siblings we have, our nationality, and where we live in our early life are just a few of the factors that make our experiences unique from one another.

Even the conditions of identical twins will vary in innumerable ways. Which twin was the larger at birth or born first, which is slightly more extrovert and attracts a little more attention from her parents? All these factors play a part, but it is not just the conditions we find ourselves in that are responsible for our own uniqueness. We are not just 'blank canvas' waiting to be drawn on by external conditions; we respond differently to a very similar set of circumstances.

Nature and nurture both impact on who we become, and so does our journey through life as our inner self meets external circumstances and is further conditioned by each of these events. Each moment, who we are thus far meets and is changed by what happens and by how we respond to it. We are like a child's old-fashioned toy kaleidoscope: with each tiny turn of the column, a new starburst of colour and formation reveals itself to the eye at the other end.

However, generally we don't experience ourselves like a kaleidoscope, with our bodies and minds changing rapidly as conditions change. We don't experience ourselves like this because we implicitly view ourselves as fixed and immutable and we're paying more attention to the concept or view of 'me' than to our direct experience. In particular, we have the view of ourselves as having some sort of core that is the real 'me'. A self. Who I am. This view of ourselves as a self is completely natural and we take it for granted. It is deeply embedded in our psyche and we wear it like a second skin.

While we have a deep-seated belief in ourselves having a 'self' that is real and permanent, we also have wildly differing emotions, opinions, and desires that would seem to belong to at least a dozen different selves! We can be deeply in love with someone and be convinced of their near perfection, but in a matter of months, or sometimes only weeks, we see our partner in a very different and much less flattering way. Sometimes the love survives the more realistic perspective, but all too often we feel let down, as if it were not our own feelings and perceptions that had fooled us into the fantasy view of another.

Our views and opinions shift, our emotions can blow a storm through us in an hour. Our perspective is constantly changing depending on a variety of external and internal factors. The only sure thing is that we are always coming from some sort of view.

Right View – a Helpful Perspective

Right View is a big topic in Buddhism, and I'll touch on it in different places through the book. Right View is both a correct understanding of the Buddha's teaching in general, and, an understanding of the doctrine or 'law' of conditionality (*paṭicca samuppāda*). Conditionality is often spoken of as cause and effect, how things come into being through the presence of certain causes and conditions and disappear when those conditions end or are absent.

It is because of the law of conditionality that we are able to lead the spiritual life. If we look after the conditions that support growth such as mindfulness, stability of mind, and wisdom, those qualities will grow. Therefore, we need to understand what those conditions are, and how to apply them. This is very much what we're exploring in this book. If we have the right conditions, there is no need to worry about the results since at some point they will become evident. If we focus on looking after the conditions, checking every now and again to make any adjustments needed, we can trust we're doing enough. One of the conditions to help wisdom come into being is the perspective of conditionality itself, which I'll talk about in this chapter as Right View.

More poetically, we can see Right View in general terms as the perspective of the Buddha: how the Buddha might have experienced things or responded to them from his Enlightened perspective. We can contrast this with our own unenlightened way of reacting to and viewing experiences in terms of self.

Given that we are always coming from one view or another, it is not such a big shift to think in terms of training in a dharma perspective or 'Right View'. With Right View we adopt a helpful perspective that is able to notice currents of thinking and emotions that are strongly influencing us, and expressed through our speech and actions. We practise being aware of whatever is arising within the body or mind from a more impersonal and objective point of view.

One example of how we do this is to get into the habit of using less personal language. We change how we speak to ourselves. We might think 'the body' rather than 'my body', or 'the breath' rather than 'I'm breathing'. The way that we speak or think to ourselves is important. We can reinforce particular habitual views or open up a more spacious mind state that allows new perspectives to be known. By itself, using more impersonal phrases is a linguistic trick that the mind soon gets used to, but when used in conjunction with practice supported by Right View it can be quite powerful.

Usually we are very involved and identified with whatever is happening to us or within us. We tend to look at whatever we do, what happens to us, or who we think we are in a highly personalized and subjective way. Central to us is the deeply held and usually implicit view that all these experiences are happening to *me*. This may seem like a no brainer; well of course, you might say. It's my body. And my mind. I think my own thoughts. Who else could they belong to? But where the notion of Right View is taking us is to ask: is that really true? How do you know that this sense of 'me' is not just yet another unquestioned view you're carrying around and assuming to be true?

If you have some Buddhist training, you might have at least a theoretical understanding that questions the view of a permanent self that is the cause and the recipient of everything that happens to it. It is helpful to have what Sayadaw U Tejaniya calls 'borrowed wisdom', which is some familiarity with and intellectual understanding of the Buddha's teachings. When we read or listen to Dharma teachings we are 'borrowing' wisdom in the form of information. When we have really taken it in, practised with it, and understood it deeply, eventually the wisdom becomes our own.

How Right View Isn't Really a View

In the early Buddhist tradition, Right View is understood in relation to two teachings: conditionality, and the doctrine of karma, which is a specific application of conditionality. Both these teachings are to do with deep insight into the nature of cause and effect and they address such questions as why things happen to us and what are the conditions that lead to something happening, or to something else stopping? The doctrine of karma is specifically concerned with our ethical behaviour: which of our intentional actions of body, speech, and mind lead to more mental suffering, and which to a decrease in suffering and a growth in happiness?

You may well be thinking at this point: why would I want to substitute my existing views for another one? And you'd have a point, although Right View has a different function to our usual views. We can see Right View as an investigative tool rather than a view in itself. It is a benign and curious perspective that enables all the other views to be known. We use the reflexive mind which allows us to mentally turn back and look at our own experience. We develop this reflexive 'muscle' so that it works with awareness, always looking to notice how something came about, rather than believe it wholesale.

When we see through the eyes of Right View, the lens we're looking through is not coloured or distorted by other habits or views but is clear and therefore able to recognize other views and attitudes in action. We use the training perspective of Right View to recognize wrong views, and through recognizing them from a more objective stance we are a little freer of them to see them for what they are.

Investigating Phenomena

Before coming to look more at how to practise with Right View in our direct experience, I want to return to the *Satipaṭṭhāna Sutta* and look at the fourth satipaṭṭhāna (being present with mindfulness or attending with mindfulness).

Right View has considerable overlap with the fourth satipaṭṭhāna; this, if you remember, is *dhammas*. The Pali word Dhamma (Dharma in Sanskrit) has a number of meanings but primarily as the teaching of the Buddha. This meaning is relevant here as *dhammas* (plural) is usually seen not as another aspect of experience like the first three satipaṭṭhānas (of body, feelings, and mind). In common with Right View it is a way of viewing our experience from the perspective of the Dharma rather than from our habitual perspectives and identities. Most significantly we're looking to see how we identify and attribute any or all of these perspectives to 'me', or as 'myself'.

Dhammas also means 'phenomena' – momentary objects or appearances or experiences. We can also talk about occurrences or happenings that are always arising. The language of *dhammas* is trying to avoid making a *thing* from a *process*, for example when we reduce the breath to one thing, 'a breath', rather than being aware of the many different sensations and processes. The breath can be made up of tickling sensations, coolness, heat, movement, dryness, and moisture, to name just a few. Some sensations we'd be hard pressed to name but we know we can feel them. It is natural when we're talking or naming our experience to use shorthand concepts like 'the breath'.

Learning to use ideas and develop language has been a hugely significant part of our human evolution, and yet to see beyond the concepts to the nature of experience we need Right View or a Dharma perspective. Concepts make sense of things for us by skimming the surface of experience to pick out familiar objects and quickly decide what or who they are. We make something of a 'best guess', which works well enough most of the time, but it is a superficial look. Mindfulness and Right View allow us to take a deeper look at what is happening in direct experience. From this perspective, we can be aware if we are relating to experience as somewhat fixed with an implicit idea of an essential core or essence, or if we are relating to it as passing momentary experiences or happenings.

When we're able to watch our senses at play we can notice a fluidity and lack of fixity in our experience. We bring mindful attending to phenomena arising within our experience through the five physical senses and the mind sense starts to 'de-clump'! Rather than automatically gravitate to concepts which fix and solidify experience, awareness is able to know the fleeting and momentary sensations associated with, for example, the body. The focus is on experience as a continuous flow or a series of happenings. It is pointing to a world and a 'self' that isn't fixed but much more fluid and alive.

Objects of Experience

> Mind can contemplate mind. The ability to make
> consciousness reflexive, to become aware that we are
> aware, to know that we know, seems to be a specifically
> human characteristic . . . the human mind has the
> capacity to turn its attention back on itself and take a
> questioning attitude even to consciousness itself.
>
> In other words, although your state of consciousness
> is subjective, when you think of it (become aware of it)
> you make it into an object – a mental object, a 'dhamma'.
> You can turn 'you' the subject into 'you' the object.
> You don't just experience sense desire (for example),
> you know that you experience it. Your desire for sense
> experience (enjoyment) is part of your subjectivity, but
> when you become aware of this desire you make it into
> an object.[3]

When we train in a Right View or a Dharma perspective, we encourage wisdom qualities to be present and 'working' in the mind. To do this, we must know what is happening, so we watch the mind with awareness.

Using the language of 'objects' in our meditation is one simple way to apply Right View without a lot of conceptual overlay. We've already being doing this in the exercises so far, but in this chapter we're taking it a bit further. We've been using that natural human function that Sangharakshita is talking about above – reflexive consciousness – and cultivating awareness. Whatever we're aware of – for example, a body sensation, a pleasant or unpleasant feeling, a thought, image, or memory in the mind – we can become conscious of it, aware of it, and know it as an 'object' arising within the field of experience.

Now we can train the mind to recognize whatever is happening through the six senses as an object arising in the mind. In exactly the same way as we lightly remind ourselves to be aware, or check that we're aware, we remind ourselves of the right view on experience; that whatever is arising is not 'me' but simply an object that can be known in awareness. This perspective enables us to see experiences more clearly and objectively. We know the object in a more impersonal way rather than seeing it through the lens of 'self' and how this object relates to 'me'.

Relating to experience with Right View will feel different to when we are more personally invested in what's happening. This could be at times when we're ill and noticing our symptoms. We can notice them in a worried, fearful way, or with some dispassion as different sensations arising, where we're able to assess how we need to act to treat ourselves. Another example is when something we do is criticized. If we take the criticism personally it will feel very painful, but when we can see it more objectively – as a shrinking contraction in the body with unpleasant feelings and various thoughts in the mind – much of the sting is taken out of it.

Bear in mind that although we will naturally notice the objects of experience, we want to also notice *how* we're aware of experience, particularly *in relation to self-view*. Our more usual way would be in the more personal and self-referential way as I've described above, where we feel (our) experiences as an implicit part of ourselves. When we've been practising with Right View for a while, we might notice we're observing more impersonally; experience is naturally known as objects arising in experience. We don't try and make this happen; it's enough to be aware of how awareness is relating to whatever is happening.

Remember that the object is less important than the awareness, and that we're looking to strengthen awareness. The object is simply something the awareness can know and we're learning to relate to the *process* of any object rather than solely the *content*. We rest with the process rather than fixating on one particular aspect of the object – for example, believing the content of a thought, rather than recognizing the process of 'thinking' is happening, that it's an activity of the mind, and how that feels in the moment. Since our bias is generally strongly towards the conceptual content, we need to consciously redirect the mind to the experience in the present moment.

Right View can help clarify the *nature* of both the object and awareness. Awareness and Wisdom are simply *knowing* all that is happening. The objects and processes through our six senses are all *being known* by awareness. Anything that happens (not *everything*, that would be exhausting and impossible!) can be known, even the smallest and subtlest of sensations or movements of mind.

Whenever we experience something, we are able to 'know' it, or be aware of it. The awareness or knowing is distinguishable from the object or what is known. Our usual consciousness doesn't make this distinction – the focus is on, for example, the car that is being seen rather than the consciousness or awareness of seeing. When there isn't much awareness there tends to be a merging in experience between consciousness and the object of consciousness. But when we practise mindfulness, we can feel quite easily the knowing quality of consciousness as well as the object.

According to Buddhism, consciousness always arises with an object which will be a manifestation of one of the six senses. We are always conscious of *something*, even if we are only dimly aware of it. As Sangharakshita says above, we have the capacity to know that we know, or be aware that we're aware. It can be interesting to explore in our experience how we are aware of both the 'knowing' side of the equation and the object that is 'being known'.

At different stages of our practice we can have different insights or understandings about the relationship between consciousness or awareness, and its objects. Sometimes there may feel something of a separation between our 'knowing' and what is 'known', and at other times there is a sense of flow, of all experience happening without a 'knower'. A phrase I've found helpful over the years, that transcends the dichotomy above, is that consciousness and object are *not separate, but they are distinguishable*. They are two sides of the same coin of the subjective and objective aspects of human consciousness.

Without the phrase above we might be tempted to side with one side of the dichotomy, considering one 'right' or more advanced spiritually. It's important, here, to remember the receptive nature of the practice and not come to a premature conclusion about the nature of our experience. This attitude can help us to continue to explore experience and allows for further insights to unfold over time.

Mindful Pause: Practising Using Right View and a Dharma Perspective – Recognizing Objects of Experience

Take some time to tune in, to check your mind and body. Relax and notice that you're breathing. Settle in the present moment, and anchor with an aspect of experience, perhaps breathing, body sensations, or sounds. Give yourself all the time in the world.

1 When you feel somewhat present to the mind and body, see if you can become aware of how you are relating to these aspects of experience – breath, body sensations, and sounds. You can do this through noticing the whole picture of what's happening, and the various thoughts and feelings about the experience that are also going on.

> Are you relating in a personal way to experiences – for example, thoughts about the sounds around you, perhaps wishing they would go away so you won't be disturbed?
> Or is there an unbiased acceptance of what is happening where you're just noticing different happenings?

2 You can also practise using the language of 'objects' towards whatever is arising in your experience. Do this lightly with curiosity, just dropping in the reminder that thoughts, sensations, feelings, and all other objects are not 'you'. They are happening on their own terms; a thought is just a thought; a body sensation is simply that. They are all objects known by awareness.

> How is it to notice the sensations of the breath as an object changing moment by moment? Or sounds as objects that awareness can know simply as sound? Or body sensations that arise, persist for a while, and then end?

You're just trying it out, using Right View to be aware of experience simply as an object, a happening within the body-mind.

Every now and again remind yourself of this perspective: you're just getting the mind used to standing back a little so you can see how it is working.

Do this as a gentle reminder. You're not trying force any change but to make clearer the perspective the mind already has.

After a while, you can open up the awareness to anything that arises within the body-mind.

When we're able to recognize the ways the mind and body are affected from a standpoint of positive detachment, we learn the art of standing in an unbiased relationship to our experience. When we can do this, even momentarily – and it may be just for a moment – we are free from the pushing and pulling that comes from identifying with what is happening. This can be subtle shifts of attitude or deep emotional swings that drag us between despair and elation. When we're aware with Right View we still feel those swings, but we know them for what they are.

We are usually deeply immersed in the habits of greed, aversion, and identification and they have their own momentum. It takes a certain mental discipline to not rush head on into the same ways of responding, with anger or blame or withdrawal, when we're upset or when we think we're right. It takes dedication, moment to moment, to build a different habit, that of awareness and patience to wait to see that bear fruit. Finally, it takes trust, or faith, that the receptive and attentive qualities of awareness and Right View will be enough. When we get a taste of the benefits of not interfering with our experience and see it clearly as simply a series of momentary arisings, the mind naturally starts to release its grip on wanting something different or something more.

Gradually, as trust is built up, the remit of awareness and Right View extends to more challenging and crucial situations. We see that the old habits, which are outdated attempts at managing and controlling our lives, are not necessary. There is a deep peacefulness in those moments of clear seeing. When we know clearly the suffering certain habits of mind lead to, then the compulsion to follow them is diminished and can eventually be extinguished.

Bhikkhu Anālayo, the wonderful teacher and writer on Satipaṭṭhāna, talks of 'de-conditioning the mind of its biases'.[4] This happens through a non-reactive observation of whatever is happening in experience. When we don't further contribute to our mental reactivity by simply becoming aware of it, like a fire deprived of fuel, sooner or later the flames decrease, the fire dies down and eventually goes out.

See How You're Relating to What's Happening

What does this mean practically? How do we translate Right View or the idea of *dhammas* and phenomena into the practice? We are training the mind to consciously adopt a way of seeing that brings to light our subjective relationship to what we experience. Right View helps take the 'I' out of experience. We could say we're training in seeing things as the Buddha would have seen them.

An important part of the practice is to notice how we are relating to any experience. The *relationship* to a sight or sound or any other sense object including thoughts and mental objects can masquerade as awareness. We think we are aware of 'seeing' but we can easily miss a mental quality of disliking or wanting that is also in the mind and affecting *how* we view the object.

Whenever we notice this happening, instead of focusing on the initial sense object, perhaps a pain in the body, *we switch our attention to the disliking*, which is an aspect of aversion, *rather than focus on the pain*. The aversion becomes the primary object of awareness. The pain sensations will still be known by the awareness, but they are now secondary to the mind object – the aversive quality in the mind. If we don't recognize the aversion in the mind it will influence the quality of the mind and start to overrun awareness. By making an object of aversion we allow the awareness to maintain a balance of helpful qualities. Both Right View and awareness contribute to this process.

We'll look more at how to work with mindfulness when there is craving or aversion in the mind in the next chapter. But seeing how you are relating to whatever is happening is very helpful for the mind and can take away a lot of the stress and tension. It can be any mind state that gets between the awareness and the object acting like a filter placed in front of a camera lens; it colours and changes how the object is seen. The colouring might be of anxiety, a stressed mental state, boredom, or desire. It might be a more helpful state such as loving kindness or peacefulness. It's equally important to be aware of these states to see the kind of influence they have on the mind, whether helpful or unhelpful.

What you may notice is how often the mind relates to experience in a personal way. You can check how that sense of ownership manifests in your experience. What sort of thoughts point you to recognizing that there's some identification with a pain in the body or in a few words of praise? You might not always notice thoughts, but instead some contraction in the body or certain feelings that you start to recognize as the sense of self making itself known.

Whether the experience is pleasing to us or not, the mind can appropriate any sort of experience to itself. You might be aware of the mind that is grasping experience or appropriating an experience. Can you bring that sense of interested awareness to what is happening in this moment? Whatever awareness and Right View can recognize is valuable. What can you learn about 'grasping' by feeling into it and being aware of it? There is no aspect of experience we're trying to make go away and nothing we are trying to get ourselves to see.

When We Understand Right View, We Understand Conditionality

The Buddha talked about this perspective as Right View. Right View refers to the kaleidoscope perspective – each moment of our lives and our experience are in constant flux. More than that, each moment conditions the next. When we wake up in a bad mood, if we're not aware of it, it's very easy for the lens of that mood to condition what happens next and deepen that state of suffering. Perhaps there's no hot water for a shower and so we snap at our housemate, assuming they are responsible for using it all. And then perhaps we're mortified when we find out that the heating system has broken down and our friend has already called the plumber out to fix it!

When we deeply understand Right View, we know in a clear and visceral sense that things don't happen because we want them to, or because the universe is for or against us, but because the causes and conditions support something happening or not happening. The bad mood has been conditioned by, for example, staying up too late and not getting enough sleep, as well as the many previous occasions where we've responded with irritation to feeling a bit under par. The shower water is cold because the boiler is broken, or because of a lack of water pressure. Our friend's thoughtlessness is just one possibility of several, not the inevitable one.

We understand that nothing is exempt from the law of conditionality, whether it is a tree growing supported by the conditions of sunlight, soil, and water, or our own minds nourished by wholesome or unwholesome qualities. External conditions like having enough food and rest and a means of financial support are helpful but they are not always within our control. To the extent we understand cause and effect we let go of trying to control things so that we get our preferred outcome and instead we focus on setting up conditions that may bring the desired result. We work on conditions in the present moment rather than try and control something happening in the future. And what we always have some degree of influence over is our own minds – how we respond or react to the 'objects' in our experience.

Implicit in the law of conditionality is the impersonal nature of conditions. We can't force something to happen, but we can influence the outcome. When we're facing an exam, we can't guarantee we'll be fit and healthy on the day, or that the questions will come from an area we've revised in, but we can prepare as best we can. Right View understands that's all we can do; there are many different factors and we only have control over a few of them.

The deepest level of understanding of conditionality, expressed in Right View, is that there is *nothing but conditions* and this includes us. Our very nature is conditioned right through and does not rest on a solid core or soul. Of course, there is continuity in our experience, sometimes to a high degree as changes in the body happen slowly over time, or as with a mental habit we think we'll never change. The teaching on conditionality doesn't deny our personality or character, it simply says they are shaped by our actions and choices and it is up to us in which direction we choose to go. This continuity allows for us take responsibility for our minds through our ethical and meditative practice.

A Wise Involvement with Objects

I want to come back to earlier in this chapter where I raised the question of whether 'intimacy with experience' is at odds with wanting to encourage a clear observation of what is happening in the mind and body. Is mindfulness really a spoilsport? Does Right View overlook the beauty inherent in our world?

One reservation I have with the language of intimacy is that it can encourage a merging into the object of experience. Absorption into the object is something you would actively encourage in meditation with a single focus, resolving in a higher, more refined consciousness, for example, the mindfulness of breathing meditation, but not in the style of practice I'm offering here.

Here we are looking to clearly know both the object and the awareness and that can't be done if the two are merged. The mind naturally has the tendency to be drawn into different sights and sounds, thoughts and other mental objects, but here we are simply looking to know any of those sights and sounds and thoughts as they are happening *and also* to clearly know the mind that is aware. We're looking to recognize awareness as an object of awareness.

Right View lends objectivity to our awareness. We are concerned with seeing experience clearly and with a certain detachment or non-attachment. However, it's not detachment from *experience* that is meant but detachment from mind states that cause suffering. In essence, we're detaching from an attachment to fulfilling our desires and rejecting what we dislike.

Right View encourages a *wise involvement* with experiences. This allows us to be aware of when our involvement with an object is one of attachment. This might reveal an attachment to a person or a view, or in my Spanish reverie, to beauty.

We're looking to view our experience without attachment influencing the observation. If we have even a little desire to be intimate with experience *because* it feels good, *because* it's pleasurable, that is desire or craving in operation.

We need to examine this idea or feeling of intimacy with the same quality of awareness as we would anything else. It can't be exempt from our observing mind or we end up with being identified with the pleasant qualities it holds. We need intimacy without identification. Wisdom can't flower in the mind that is attached and identified.

Yet. Paradoxically, something about the *experience* of non-identified awareness, whether of a sight or sound, emotion or thought, often has the flavour of presence, delicacy, richness, and curiosity. Less involvement in states of craving leads to a greater satisfaction. Ironically, this can feel very much like a kind of intimacy!

Wisdom Doing Its Own Work

It's not necessary to try and change the perspective from one where there is more identification with an aspect of body or mind through any of the senses. It's not the job of awareness to make experience different but just to recognize what is actually there. However, the more we remind ourselves of the training perspective, the more we'll notice over time an unbiased flavour to the mind that is observing. There will be a decrease in judging or resisting the experience, or perhaps an absence of infatuation with it. This may be a gradual process or may completely change the state of mind at times. It depends on how clearly the mind is 'knowing' the experience for what it is.

Rather than 'my sore knee' and a degree of involvement in the story and anxious thoughts about it (will it clear up for me to run the half marathon next month? maybe I shouldn't meditate for long, it might make it worse), we'll be aware of all of it. This includes the sensations of discomfort, perhaps some thoughts and bodily feelings that we'd recognize as anxiety. The difference will be that the awareness is not caught up and identified with them. The observing mind will be relaxed and aware of each experience with an unbiased and curious mind.

When we're able to observe experience without trying to change it we're allowing *wisdom to do its own work*. It's the work of observing the mind and its interrelationship with the physical senses, from a perspective that is less subjective. You might recognize that 'wrong view' rather than 'right view' is present when you're noticing identifying bodily pain with 'me'.

Seeing 'Wrong View' is 'Right View'

The fact that you are able to recognize wrong view operating in the mind means that you are aware of it from the perspective of 'right view'. This is a deeply encouraging perspective. Whatever you observe is contributing to seeing a bigger picture that, little by little, frees the mind from mental and emotional bondage. Seeing the bondage clearly is itself part of the process of the knots untying and falling away.

The same is true whenever we are able to notice what we can call *the feeling of me* – it is worth remembering that this is Right View in action. Even though we are observing a habitual view of self which in itself is a deeply conditioned wrong view, what is new is that we are able to recognize it. We can only recognize it because we're viewing the experience from the perspective of Right View. It is worth celebrating those moments when we're aware of 'selfing' since the mind can only notice them because of the presence of awareness and Right View!

When we're able to see what's happening calmly and clearly there is a positive detachment which contributes to a lack of identification with the knots themselves. We might still feel the mental pressure or restriction but we're not *inside* it in the same way. This means, in that moment, we're not driven by those habits which tend to take a lot of our energy and focus. Awareness and Right View work with a broad, open mind quality which leaves energy free to notice what else is happening.

Recognizing When We Identify with Experience

When we don't identify with an aspect of our experience as 'self' or 'not self/me', we allow a subtle, yet quite monumental shift. We're able to see how we create our own suffering but without being lost in dis-ease or dissatisfaction. We can't control this shift in perspective, we can't make it happen, though we can influence its arising more frequently. We can train our minds to remember Right View and to notice, whenever we're able, whether the mind is relating to experience in an objective, or subjective and identified way.

When I reflected back on my experience driving through the blossoming almond trees, I came to a different conclusion. What I thought was wisdom seeing more objectively was more likely the mind coloured by greed that had seeped into the pleasurable experience. The desire for the pleasure to continue meant wisdom couldn't work properly in the mind. The feeling of diminished pleasure was craving reacting to mindfulness as a party pooper!

But there have been other experiences over time where seeing craving for what it is – a momentary arising in the mind – has been more satisfying than the initial pleasure of the object. In those moments there has been some wisdom in the mind that is able to appreciate reality rather than feel disappointed by it.

In the next chapter, we'll extend the reach of Right View, or a Dharma or wisdom perspective. We will focus on the mind that tries to draw within what it desires, and conversely, the aversive mind which rejects or pushes away. Rather than make us happy, these two modes of craving and aversion are a direct line to our suffering, and this suffering or *dukkha* is where we will start.

Mindful Pause: Knowing Whatever Arises as an Object within Experience

Take time to allow the mind to settle and for awareness to stabilize, and enjoy being present.

Use the Right View perspective to explore how you are relating to any thoughts, emotions, physical sensations, sounds, and sights (as well as tastes and smells).

Are you relating to your experience simply as impersonal objects arising into experience through the different sense doors?

Or is the experience more subjective, more personal, and somewhat 'sticky' or unclear?

Either state – right view or wrong view – can be known in awareness for what it is. Initially, you just want to get a sense of the difference between subjective and objective.

If you don't know, that's fine. You don't need to try too hard to find out. Just notice what's happening in the next moment of experience.

You can also use Right View to notice more clearly experience that points to a view of self.

Can you sense 'I' in the thoughts and mental activity, either explicitly or implicitly?

This might be through being aware of a presence you know as 'me' or noticing thoughts and feelings about 'me'. Or some feeling in the body that indicates some ownership or identification with an experience.

Keep in mind that the investigation is about awareness rather than thinking. See what awareness can know while keeping a light, open quality of mind.

Can you notice when emotions reference back to a sense of self? 'I'm sad' or 'I'm so disappointed'. How is it to notice them as more impersonal 'objects' arising in the mind?

Regularly remind yourself of the Right View – you're looking to know experience as 'objects' – so that view starts to hover in the back of your mind as a new way of seeing.

Mindful Life Moment: A Modern-day Anatomical Parts Practice

I was recently fortunate enough to be on retreat with Bhikkhu Anālayo studying and practising the *Satipaṭṭhāna Sutta*. We were introduced to a meditation practice where, before each period of open, unstructured awareness, Anālayo led us through several body scans. The first three scans were an abbreviated form of what's known as the 'Anatomical Parts' practice. The Buddha likens the parts of the body to different types of grains such as rice and barley, held in a bag (i.e. skin). Each day we scanned through the body, noting 'skin', then 'flesh', and in the third scan, 'bones'.

The practice came back into my mind at a recent visit to the dentist.

The thought of a visit to the dentist used to fill me with anxiety and tension. 'Don't be silly', I remember the unsympathetic, white-coated woman saying as she prepared to stick a needle into my nine-year-old gums. All I'd done was unconsciously take a sharp in breath and a death grip on the arms of the plastic chair I was lying rigid in.

Over the years of adulthood, with better dentists and many years of spiritual practice, the experience has changed. Watching my mind means I'm able to observe habitual fear and aversion before it gets too much of a hold. I'm able to relax and notice other things – the lights, sounds, close contact with another human being – rather than contract around a single unpleasant object (pain). Generally speaking, these days I'm pretty calm going into the chair.

As I write, I'm at home following minor dental surgery – an implant at the back of my mouth. Apart from a small tear at the corner of my mouth there is no discomfort at all.

Despite some initial apprehension (watching thoughts the day of the surgery as they focused around what might go wrong), I found the experience quite interesting. The dentist was pretty good at telling me what was going to happen, but I realized he was also leaving things out, presumably for my benefit!

The first time I didn't know what was happening was feeling a scraping in my mouth and realizing it could not be the familiar sound of metal instrument against tooth. There was no longer a tooth there, so the sound had to be metal on bone . . . which meant the shoving and pulling of the previous ten minutes had been the cutting and scraping back of my gums! Whoah!

There followed a few 'burr holes' into the bone of my upper jaw to establish the best line to angle the implant 'post'. The bone was unusually dense, so the vibrations caused by the drill intensified, and crackling sounds and sensations, like a car driving on gravel, spat out at regular intervals.

After much deliberation and several X-rays, the post was screwed with by what I imagined was a tiny dental spanner, each twist securing the post into the drilled hole. Finally, the retracted gums were sewn back together with several stitches. I caught glimpses of the black thread coming into my field of vision and felt the pinprick of the needle. All this happened within an hour and a half of much pushing and shoving of my mouth and cricking of my neck.

While all this was going on, I was aware of different levels of 'happenings'. I was aware of wanting to make the procedure go as quickly and smoothly as possible. My mouth was readily open as wide as I could manage, I lay still and worked against the choking sensations of water, not caught by the suction pipe, hitting my throat. I was as model a patient as I could be!

I was also aware of some reflections in the mind noticing the resonances between the procedure and daily life. Wrenches, spanners, needle, and thread all seemed part of a different world – one I'm becoming more familiar with as a new homeowner. How could the same objects and concepts used for hemming curtains and bleeding radiators be now digging into my precious flesh and bone? I was amused by the mental second takes that tried to make sense of this. I've watched plenty of *Grey's Anatomy* in my time, with its fictional digging around in human bodies, but that's not the same as having the same thing happening to my own.

I was also noticing the thoughts, views, and feelings around that mental perturbation. The surgery was a minor assault on 'self', invading beyond the boundary of skin and flesh. It was also an opportunity to see where ideas of 'me' and 'mine' were hiding out. There was a sense that going beyond skin and cutting into flesh was not only an invasion of 'self' but that skin, flesh, and bones were themselves hiding the reality of what I take to be 'me'. The notion of me was challenged when usually unseen parts were cut open and drilled into and then sewn up again.

Watching all of this, I was keyed back into the mind-set of Anālayo's retreat. The body scans that set up our sitting practice were there to facilitate an attitude of detachment – an aspect of Right View. And that I could observe the mind at ease, aware of subtle resistances and protestations, showed me that there was some degree of detachment there – as well as some degree of attachment! But, hey, wisdom was working in the mind to some extent.

Detachment and wisdom are friends to awareness, allowing the mind to observe more of its own workings. And the mind that is aware and curious can use any object to investigate its own nature. Eventually, the mind starts to intuit its own 'nature' and realize there is nothing to hold on to.

Chapter five

The Cycle of Suffering

> Objects are always changing; therefore, consciousness is
> always moving, tottering, impermanent, changing and
> becoming otherwise.[1]

We all know the scenario: we want to practise, to meditate regularly,
to be aware more of the time, and be a kinder, wiser person. And yet
there are times, maybe more frequent than we'd like to admit, when
we do just the opposite. We sleep in and then don't get around to
meditating, days go by without much awareness, and despite our
best intentions we act and speak in ways that betray our values or
hurt others.

We can say 'that's just the way it is', or we can feel slightly guilty
about our habits, but it is worth being curious about *why*, at times,
we can't stick to our intentions. What is it that gets in the way when
we have the right information and externally conducive conditions
to practise or to live well? We can talk about it in terms of a lack of
integration and that would be accurate. Part of us wants to practise
and the other part prefers to lie in or consume junk food or trashy
novels and let slip impatient comments. There is a tension between
how we are and how we want to be which can be very painful and
frustrating.

Curiosity can help us step back from this scenario and see what
receptive awareness with Right View (dharma perspective) can offer.
Let's start with looking at some other perspectives implicit in Right
View, known as the *three characteristics* (*lakkhaṇas/lakṣaṇas* – Pali/
Sanskrit).

Life Isn't Fair! (*Dukkha*)

As far as the Buddha was concerned, it all starts with *dukkha*; dis-ease or dissatisfaction. The Pali word *dukkha* is also translated as 'suffering', which can be the case at times, but is perhaps too strong a word for the subtlety of the experience. *Dukkha* ranges from physical pain and discomfort to an almost imperceptible existential disquiet. Even within those times when we are enjoying ourselves, we can sometimes have the feeling that something is not quite right. We may not be able to pin down that feeling, though sometimes there might be anxiety that the enjoyable activity is finite and at some point it will end, and we don't want that. Or there may be a slight disappointment that the long-anticipated event doesn't quite live up to our internal hype.

Having said that, the teaching of *dukkha* does not deny that there are times when we're happy and content. All it is saying is that it won't last. Sooner or later, we'll rub up against 'life' in a way that brings about suffering. Even with the best of lives it is inevitable that sometimes we'll suffer and feel that life is just not fair!

When we're happy and content with our lives it is easy to forget about *dukkha*. Life is good, until once again it is not. And so, we put more effort into trying to bring close all the things that are precious to us. We look to bolster ourselves against the insecurity we feel from our dis-ease. We don't see that *dukkha* is built into the nature of everything in the world, including our own bodies and minds. Resisting the suffering that comes from change is like trying to resist the weather; if the conditions are there, say, a warm front and low pressure, rain is almost inevitable.

This doesn't mean we don't shelter from the weather or take a raincoat and umbrella to avoid getting wet. In the same way, we have choices about how we respond to what presents itself to us. We can resist and put ourselves in opposition to what's happening by trying to ignore or control the situation, or we can flow with it, like a stick floating downstream, working *with* the conditions we find ourselves in. Whether it be a difficult manager at work, a frail parent to look after, or our own habitual mental state of resistance to practise, we always have some degree of choice.

Empty of Self Nature (*Anattā*)

The Pali word *anattā* is closely connected to *dukkha*. It is usually translated as 'not self'. To put a big idea very simply, it says that the experience of 'me' isn't dependent on a fixed core or central reference point. You'll remember that we've already been working with this concept in the previous chapter on Right View. Training the mind to recognize 'objects' arising in experience is to start to disentangle sense experiences from the awareness that knows them. Within that, we start to have insights into the nature of self, and we can naturally see the sense of self when it arises as simply another idea in the mind.

Anattā doesn't deny what is sometimes a high degree of continuity – for example, in the natural world of mountains or rivers, or in a person. Sure, over time I change but I look roughly the same each morning when I look in the bathroom mirror. *Anattā* recognizes the relative stability of things, and of character, but not the existence of a soul, a self, or 'consciousness in charge'. There are simply conditions, habits, and tendencies formed into a personality over time. There is continuity and relationship between a seed and the tree it grows into, but there is nothing outside of the relationship between several conditions that brought the 'tree' into full growth. It is the same for living beings.

Who Is in Charge?

A further implication of *anattā* relevant here is 'ungovernable'. This conveys to me quite beautifully how we put ourselves in opposition to what is actually happening. We think we are *self-g*overning. Even if we know we don't have control in the external world, we still have the illusion of it internally. We feel we are in charge of ourselves and it is often quite threatening to feel our lack of agency, for example when we're bossed around by a spouse or manager. We have derogatory words for when we see others lose their own sense of agency; they are henpecked, nagged, or browbeaten.

If we look at our experience, it is quite easy to see our lack of governance. As we saw at the beginning of this chapter, we just have to look at our habits, particularly the ones we're not happy with and would like to change. We break the diet even when we know how our excess weight impacts on our health, or we watch more TV despite having decided we wouldn't because it fills our minds for meditation the next day. Or we get into an argument with someone and despite our best intentions we tell them some home truths that hurt.

We tell ourselves one thing and do another. The evidence is right there that what we think of as 'me' is ungovernable. But we get around this truth by blaming our weak willpower, or the other person for provoking us. We manage to attribute our failure of control to a failure to control *ourselves*, rather than seeing from a certain perspective there is nothing to control or govern. It is not surprising we find ways to make sense through our limited perspective, as the view of self is so deeply hard-wired into our experience from infancy. Unless Right View is present, anything that happens is simply attributed to, and seen from within, the perspective of oneself.

Change Is Inevitable (*Anicca*)

Anattā (not self) and *dukkha* (dissatisfaction) are woven together with a third factor, *anicca* or impermanence. Because the nature of experience is to change, we suffer through our attachment to the idea of a fixed self, especially when things change in ways we don't want them to.

It is a given that things change; we all know this on an intellectual level. We know that things change within us and in the world around us. Sometimes the changes come slowly, as with coastal erosion, and sometimes with lightning speed, like our moods. We think we know all this and yet we don't know it very deeply. Change takes us by surprise, as when a row of houses fall into the sea or someone we love leaves us. Our understanding of impermanence is mostly intellectual, and therefore superficial, and, especially when ill health, loss, or bereavement are involved, we often are quite bewildered by it. We realize we haven't understood the nature of change at all.

It is often easier to see these universal laws (of nature) of impermanence and insubstantiality in the world outside than in our own mind and body. We marvel at inanimate objects like boulders worn smooth from the weather, or I notice the stains and nicks, through years of use, in the wooden desk I'm sitting at. But we are no different, and change – particularly changes to our bodies – can be clearly recognized with just a little awareness.

Just last week, in a moment of distractedness from my purpose (cycling in a straight line) I fell off my bike and broke my collar bone. The amount of change that has resulted from this one moment of inattention has been striking. I have become one-handed physically, many tasks take more time to complete (one-fingered typing), and some things are not possible (unscrewing lids from jars, cutting up my food). Mentally, this has produced a lot of disorientation as the mind also has to relearn how to do things, such as dressing in a way that induces the least amount of pain, or setting up conditions that make teaching possible, such as needing a sofa. Awareness has new objects: there is discomfort in new places to observe, and noticing the speed with which the mind becomes protective of this broken bone it can't see (except on an X-ray) or know directly.

When we are aware and watching our minds, we have an opportunity to see change happening in every moment: flickering body sensations with qualities of pressure, temperature, and movement; streams of thoughts that break up into words; and even more fragmentary and fleeting impressions formed of feelings, perceptions, and intentions. It's important we don't take any *experience* of change to be the same as deeply *understanding* impermanence. Experiences will come and go but understanding will turn upside down what we think we've known until then.

When awareness and wisdom are working in the mind we can see clearly the lack of stability in our experience, and by extension in others and the world around us. Things change form and move into something else, or they disappear altogether. It is this instability that is a source of suffering to us. When things are unstable, we don't feel whole or secure and our natural human tendency is to try and control what's happening.

It's important to be aware of this important Dharma idea but not to try and impose it onto our experience. It is so easy for the mind to mould concepts to fit its own view; before you know it, *anicca* or *anattā* has become something the mind has appropriated so as to feel comfortable with it. By using awareness to stay with our direct experience we learn from the inside, and at some point the learning will bear fruit.

What the Buddha Saw

Recently I was walking along a beach on the Welsh coast enjoying the sounds of the waves and the feel of the water on my feet, and the rich blues of the sky and sea. As I got closer to the nearby village, I saw many sandcastles that had been built during the day, some simple and modest and others grand affairs with multiple turrets. Each had a moat that was opened to catch the sea as it swished up the beach. The waves were small but insistent, and I was struck by one child of about eight years old desperately working alone against time and nature to stop his sandcastle being washed away by the incoming tide. He moved quickly on his knees, shovelling dry sand and working continuously to rebuild the soaked and sinking walls of his fragile castle. It struck me as a poignant metaphor for life and I felt gratitude well up that I had learned another way, however imperfectly I practised it, to be with the shifting sands of experience.

Part of the Buddha's understanding was to see the fruitlessness of trying to shore up our world, seeking lasting stability. He saw an alternative to trying vainly to create security either through yet more sense comforts or desperate attempts at controlling things beyond that were never in our control in the first place.

His approach was to turn the attention inwards and be curious about what was happening within his own body and mind. He saw that when the mind was stable enough, he could watch what was happening with a receptive objectivity. He was able to notice that some thoughts led to more mental suffering and others to a lessoning of suffering and greater freedom. Amongst the thoughts that conduced to more suffering or dis-ease were those that arose from a non-acceptance of the suffering itself.

The Buddha saw that by struggling against certain experiences he created more suffering for himself. And when he let go of the struggle his mind and body became more peaceful. Continuing with this investigative quality of mind and examining the cause-and-effect relationships between thoughts, emotions, and body sensations, he saw two main conspirators whose reactions to the inherent unsatisfactoriness and instability of things led to more *dukkha*:

- First, when we want something pleasant and enjoyable in our experience to continue. The Buddha called this craving or 'wanting'.
- And second, when we wish that something unpleasant or difficult would stop. We know this as aversion or 'not wanting'.

These two factions tug on our being, arguing with the reality of how things are, often showing up for us in bodily tension and conflicted emotions. In addition, they can cause friction in our relationships with others when what we desire is in conflict with what *they* want. Despite these unpleasant side effects, we don't see any other option but to continue, as best we can, soldiering on to get what we think we need to make us feel secure and whole.

As practitioners, we know we *do* have an alternative, but habits are strong with roots that go deep into our ways of being: pleasure = good and right so I must have more, and unpleasant = bad and wrong, so I must try and make it go away. This may seem a little simplistic, but the implicit message spelled out here is encoded into our deepest and most instinctual survival mechanisms. And they've worked – we've survived! But spiritual growth is about more than survival and the Buddha's insight into the causes of suffering makes clear for us the path to greater peace, happiness, and freedom.

Through practising awareness and Right View we get to know craving and aversion and how they manifest in the mind and body. There is a third factor that conditions *dukkha* and that is ignorance, sometimes called delusion, and we'll go into that in chapter 7. Delusion, craving, and aversion are broad-brush terms that cover all emotions and mind states that lead to suffering. These are sometimes called afflictive emotions or 'poisons' as they often cause pain or harm to the mind.

Our often-used strategy to deal with any sort of suffering, including uncomfortable emotions, is to try and distract ourselves with something nice. The Dharma teacher Pema Chodron famously said that this strategy might work for the small things, but pizza is pretty useless as consolation when someone you love has died. Awareness and Right View is an alternative where we come to realize there are creative alternatives to suffering other than trying to ignore difficulties by running from one desirable thing to another.

Objects Are Not the Enemy

Even though craving and aversion cause us suffering, it's important to understand we are not trying to make them go away. They are simply conditioned mind states like any other, and we want to understand rather than banish them. We're learning how to recognize craving and aversion (and their relatives) as objects arising in the mind. Right View, awareness, and objectivity are our friends in this process, along with a patient persistent effort and a curious mind.

This doesn't mean we don't *feel* the craving or aversion – we do. But we are less lost in the subjective desire – whether for another person, to get a good exam result, or for a cream cake – or its opposite – when we're angry at someone who disagrees with our great idea, or who cuts us up on the road. We can be interested in the 'nature' of craving and aversion and feel out what they are like in our experience. We learn more about them through an attitude of interested calm and a willingness to remind ourselves over and again to remember to be aware.

We can see these objects of craving and aversion from a standpoint of wisdom rather than delusion, so that they no longer have the power to agitate and proliferate suffering in the mind. We open the door to a new way of seeing and living.

Qualities That Perfume the Mind

There are, of course, positive and skilful emotions like *mettā* (loving kindness), compassion, generosity, positive remorse (after wrongdoing), and trust and confidence. As we become more aware of afflictive emotions, they have less power over us, and we live more in the orbit of positive emotions. It is equally important to notice skilful qualities in the mind, functioning in the awareness. The lens we look through can be coloured by patience, calm, or joy or any of the other helpful qualities of mind. It's important to understand the effect these positive qualities have on the mind for two reasons.

First, we're able to see within our direct experience what the effect of (for example) joy is on the mind. Does it lighten and brighten the mind? Does the awareness feel more keen and able to stay with the simple noticing of objects? Without making any assumptions, we can notice whether these skilful emotions help or hinder our ability to be aware.

Second, it is easy for the mind to become attached to and identified with qualities it enjoys, and positive emotions are mostly very pleasant to experience. With Right View, *we learn to recognize when the mind is enjoying the pleasure rather than being aware of it!* If you find, when you're meditating, you've quickly moved from enjoyment to disappointment it may be because you've been attached to the experience being a certain (pleasurable) way and resist that when it inevitably changes.

A Note of Warning

It's crucial to bear in mind, as we discuss these mental factors, that although they may feel uncomfortable to experience, they are not wrong. We may have ideas in the mind that we need to get rid of the various manifestations of craving and aversion, and a lot of our ethical practice may hinge around not acting out states of greed or irritation. I'd like to make a distinction here about how we speak and act, and how we work with our minds. The ethical training precepts work as a container for how we behave and communicate in relation to others. They are a form of positive restraint and an ongoing practice for most of us.

But the Buddha talked of other forms of positive restraint, including 'restraint by mindfulness' and 'restraint by wisdom', and this is how we are working within this practice. Our actions of body, speech, and mind are still informed by the ethical guidelines, but we allow the mind a bit more latitude. The unskilful mental factors of greed and aversion are 'held' in the container of awareness and wisdom. We learn to be with potentially strong unskilful mental states without identifying with them. We see how they manifest energetically in the body and how various thoughts will either inflame or calm them. The aim is to understand the *nature* of them so that eventually they no longer arise.

If you are familiar with the various traditional antidotes to the unskilful qualities that 'hinder' the mind from settled calm and stability, the first instruction is to *be aware* of what's happening. You would then usually move on to more active counter-measures to reduce the hindrance. In this practice, however, we stay with that first action to just be mindful of what it is in the mind. It is in this area that awareness is tested: can the spaciousness of mindful equanimity simply 'know' mental discomfort in the form of longing or rage in the mind? It is much easier to sink into the pleasurable state of longing, or to go with the flare-up into anger, especially when habits are strong. Awareness in these moments can feel deeply counter-intuitive, but when we are able to simply be mindful and feel the effects of relief or peacefulness in the mind we get a taste of where the practice is going.

The Judging Mind – a Further Word of Warning!

Strictly speaking, the judging quality of mind comes under the aversion or 'not wanting' section later in this chapter, but it is such a strong habit (which can be applied equally to craving states) that I'll mention it briefly here.

The judging mind is different to the act of discernment and the ability to discriminate. These latter qualities help clarify what is happening in the mind and are a support to awareness and wisdom. The judging quality of mind is more often harmful to the mind because of its basic aversive stance to whatever is happening. Its nature is to judge, in the sense of condemn and criticize, and whether we are judging ourselves or others it is a painful mind state to be regularly visited by.

The judging mind says 'this shouldn't be happening', 'this is wrong'. There is a non-acceptance of the experience, whatever it is. It might be that the mind is falling into fantasy, or there is restlessness while sitting. From a judgement perspective, this is wrong and should be changed, but from the point of view of awareness, 'fantasy' or 'restlessness' are simply objects to be known.

It's very helpful to be aware every time you notice 'judging' in the mind. You might catch the judgemental thoughts and be aware of the feeling in the mind that arises with judgement. Perhaps you can recognize what is happening in the body: is there a growing tightness or tension? Where do you feel these sensations? What does 'judging' feel like in the mind when we get to know it from the perspective of awareness and wisdom? Does making an object of 'judging' alter it in some way?

One last thing here: remember not to judge the judging! Judging is not wrong either. It is simply a mind state acting in line with its own nature. Judging judges, that is its function. It's not a useful one generally and will often lead to suffering when we identify with it, so keep in mind to spot it as early as you can.

Craving (*Lobha*)

Greed is inevitable in the absence of an inner aim.[2]

Now we'll take a closer look at the effect of the poisons on the mind and how we can work with them through our practice of awareness.

Each poison has a whole group or 'family' of associated emotions and mind states. The *craving* group, for example, includes *desiring, fantasizing, yearning, obsessing, intoxication, attachment, ambition,* and *greed*! And if that wasn't enough, *competitiveness, expectations,* and *comparing* yourself to others are also forms of craving that can cause us a lot of suffering.

Although the family has a common flavour of 'wanting', each manifestation of craving will have a slightly different quality to it. Each can be felt out in the body and noticed in the mind. It's not necessary to try and identify everything in the list. It is more helpful to start with what you are actually experiencing; sooner or later you'll no doubt experience many different facets of the wanting mind. It is amazing how ubiquitous the wanting mind is, and it is clearly not for nothing that the Buddha identified insight into craving (he included aversion as the other side of the same coin) as such a significant part of practice.

Our experience of body and mind become the laboratory through which we can see how these 'poisons' appear. We develop our own vocabulary to describe them. Perhaps you notice that 'greed' feels sticky to the mind, or intoxication is fizzy like champagne and easily hooks us into fantasy. You might notice that sometimes craving is primarily known through thoughts and thinking, and at other times through physical sensations and emotional yearning. There is much to be interested in, but even here it's important to notice the 'lens' you're looking through. Is it interest in being known or has curiosity been hijacked by over-eagerness and a desire to get something out of the practice?

The 'objects' of the wanting mind will often be sense objects arising from the enjoyable sounds, sights, tastes, smells, and touch sensations we notice and often reach out to. There are also the mental objects such as when the mind goes over and over a lovely day out, squeezing the juice of satisfaction out of it. Or when we want to be approved of or want to be right. And sometimes we can be aware of wanting to 'be', to be-come into the next moment, a basic clinging to existence.

Expectations

A common manifestation of craving in our meditation comes in the form of expectations. We can be quite identified with expectations because we can assume they're a good thing. We put energy into our practice with some idea in the mind of what *we want* to happen: we want to get more concentrated, or we spend time in reflection because *we want* insight to arise. If we don't recognize the craving element, we often end up paying more attention to an imagined result rather than what's happening. We can find ourselves looking for a particular experience rather than being open to what is happening in our present moment experience. When we unconsciously have an end result in mind, our goal orientation can close down other possibilities. It is hard to surprise yourself when you think you already know!

It can be helpful to distinguish between the desire to practise and the desire for a result. Both are led by desire, but wanting a result is more likely to be craving. The desire to practise tends to be present-moment led, and with wisdom at the helm. I find it interesting that not all desire comes from the poison of craving. The wisdom mind wants too but the desire there comes from a genuine wish to practise in a simple way. The wisdom mind recognizes that if you attend to the causes and conditions the effects are guaranteed. You can't say when or what the effect will look like and the wisdom mind is not so bothered about those things. When the conditions are ripe, the results – the insights – will come.

Another difference between the wanting mind and the wisdom mind is that wanting led by craving always comes from self-interest. It's all about what benefits *me* and those who are important *to me*. The wisdom mind has a much wider circle of concern. Its motivation is more objective and not self-referential because it understands the limited and provisional nature of 'self'. Instead wisdom acts from the question, 'What is best for this situation?' With openness of mind and heart, wisdom meets compassion to act in a way that is of benefit to others.

This doesn't mean we can't think about the goal of the spiritual life; study and reflection are important elements on the path. But we can hold the goal lightly in the back of the mind and try to practise without focusing on the end point.

Disenchantment

We can find ourselves coming up against a lot of resistance to investigate moments of craving. We have such an inbuilt attraction to pleasure, and it can feel so 'right', that our natural inclination is to go along with it without noticing or questioning it. We have phrases that convince us of its naturalness and innocence, like 'a little bit of what you fancy won't hurt you' or 'all things in moderation'. Whether we have a little or a lot of something is not the point; we're less interested in the object. Our aim is to see greed (*lobha*) as greed and understand its influence on our mind and life.

What can help is to notice views and feelings that we hold in relation to craving. In my own investigations, I remember discovering I held the view that life would be boring if I didn't have my little pleasures. My experience would be lacking in some way. The mind felt dull and a bit low at the thought of not acting on cravings.

I saw that I depended on 'treats' to lift my mood, rather than using Dharma practice to change the quality of my mind. The content of the view sounds rather gross as I write it here though it was well disguised. But the awareness that caught the view through various thoughts and images was quick and subtle. A whole domino line of views fell through continuous awareness, revealing the extent to which the mind was siding with craving rather than wisdom.

A further realization for me, in this area, was not only the view that my life would be lacking through not indulging in sense pleasures, but that *I* wouldn't be much fun without them! There was a fear of being seen to be a killjoy, a dour characterless Buddhist. I saw I was identified with being perceived in a certain way, and I was buying into a belief that eating certain things made 'me' a fun person. Seeing this rather odd way of thinking was instrumental in having a good laugh about it and seeing through it.

The important thing here is not whether I indulge in my sense pleasure of choice every now and again but whether I'm able to use awareness to gain some understanding. By seeing the objects of our longing *as objects* we start to break the habit of enchantment with them. The job of greed is to keep the *longing feeling in the mind* going for as long as it can. The objects really are secondary to the pleasure that the mind experiences. We think it is the creamy ice cream or the lover's touch or the colleague's approval that we crave, but we've got it all wrong. Those things are simply means to the happy or satisfied mind. And when we've practised a while, we get familiar with other ways to make the mind happy.

It's Not About the Object

A number of years ago I started what I called my 'craving project' in order to learn more about what was happening in the mind when I thoughtlessly reached out for biscuits in the supermarket, or automatically had cake when out for coffee with a friend. There were several learnings from this time that remain with me, to some degree.

I was clear at the outset that I wanted to watch my mind rather than attempt to control it. I knew I would prefer it if I didn't do certain things (like watch various things on TV or read quite so many thrillers and police procedurals) or eat so many sweet things. However, I knew from long experience that trying to persuade myself not to do these things, or setting myself precepts, might work for a while but I usually relapsed. Basically, it didn't work for me. So, I wanted to use awareness and wisdom to see what was going on. I wanted to be more interested in the process rather than fixed on an outcome.

I decided to trust my mind more. I was clear that a successful outcome was not defined by whether I succeeded in 'resisting' the desired object. I didn't want resistance to be any more important than any other factor of mind I was noticing or make resistance something I pitted 'myself' against. I realized how important it was to stay with the mind and not go to the object. Time and time again I'd notice the mind was pulled to the fantasy, imagining myself with the chocolate/ beer/entertainment. I would remind myself of Right View to help reinforce the idea that the mind was recognizing an image of a treat, or a feeling of anticipation or pleasure, whatever it was. Back-and-forth awareness would go between the mind and the object.

Taking the Long View

A couple of occasions stand out from this period. One involved a summer evening cycling back from a long and tiring day at work. I generally find cycling quite helpful to awareness and I was clearly aware the mind was seeking out perceived compensation for the day and subsequent flat mood. The treats took the form of images of me watching a movie and eating a takeaway, instead of cooking. Then the mind alighted on a mental image of the off-licence on my way home and purchasing a bottle of lager.

I was aware of craving in relation to the image and of how pleasing its longing quality felt to the mind. Simultaneously, I was aware of the awareness that was knowing craving and how that mind state was unusually luminous and satisfying. I went back and forth between the wanting mind and this luminous awareness, feeling out the quality of each. Even though I was clear the aware mind was more satisfying, I didn't know if it would win out over the seductive longing on this occasion, but I had a strong sense that eventually it would. I knew at some point there would be enough wisdom in the mind to make a clear choice not to act on craving. Right until I pulled up my bike outside the off-licence, I didn't know which way the mind would go. That evening I enjoyed a beer with my movie!

Moving on several years to the end of a period of five months' retreat in Myanmar, I was spending a few days in a magical bamboo cabin overlooking palm trees, a wide sandy beach, and the Bay of Bengal. Much of the time I simply sat on my little balcony looking at the ocean. All around me in the other cabins and at the local restaurant were people enjoying a beer or glass of wine. I felt very content with no need of anything to supplement my mind state in this little corner of paradise.

However, I did find myself looking to the future and reflecting on the question – did I want to drink alcohol again? Having invested so much time, energy, and money to get me to Myanmar, it came home to me how much I had been investing in awareness. I had been prioritizing awareness for many years, culminating in this recent extended period of practice on retreat. Did I really want to go back to doing something that, by its nature, was prioritizing unawareness? Even without feeling any effects of alcohol, as I rarely drank enough to notice, I didn't want to go with the *intention* to intoxication or lack of awareness.

The decision to not to drink alcohol felt very natural and I've only done so on a couple of occasions over the past five years. There is usually a non-alcoholic sparkly equivalent on family and other celebratory events, which suits me fine.

To my mind, the initial cycling across the park moment and the post-retreat decision are connected with each other, and with many other moments of craving seen in awareness lying between them. There was a process that couldn't be controlled by an act of will but that happened because the conditions supported it. Those conditions were mainly awareness and Right View, and faith in the effect of repeated moments of awareness and clear seeing.

Mindful Pause: Watching the Mind with Greed

We want to be aware of when greed or aversion are in the mind and bring a spacious, open awareness to these times. We want to get familiar with what 'wanting' feels like in the body and mind, or 'not wanting', when we're pushing away something we don't want.

Eating: mostly we choose what we eat and therefore we end up eating what we like (or at least what we think is good for us!).

Treat the first couple of minutes of a meal as a meditation. Before you start to eat, just look at your food, notice 'seeing' and 'smelling'. Do this is a relaxed way, aware of what else is going on around you.

See if you can notice hunger sensations, perhaps in your belly. How do you know you're hungry?

What happens when 'looking' is happening? Are there any thoughts or feelings when you're looking at the food? Are you attracted to some foods more than others when you look at them?

Notice any 'desire to eat'. What does that feel like in the mind?

Go back and forth between any feeling of physical hunger and the desire to eat felt in the mind. Play with these different 'natures' of body and mind.

When you're ready, eat your meal but stay lightly aware of the physical senses of smelling, tasting, and seeing as well as watching the mind.

Mindful Life Moment: The Ugly Pole of *Lobha*

On retreat recently, I found myself near the back of the lunch queue which stretched out of the dining hall into the corridor. I was aware (but not aware enough, as it turns out) of some restlessness and impatience as I neared the massive saucepans of hot food which were laid out on a small table. I was eager for my turn and, as I stood in line, more of my interest resided in some near future tucking into lunch than with what was happening in the present moment.

What prompted a return to awareness of the present was noticing the mind had focused on someone at the food table. He was slow to pick up his plate and so there was already a gap opening up in the queue, leaving the pans of food unattended. My mind huffed a little – how inefficient, couldn't he hurry up a bit so we could all get our food? Then, realizing he'd forgotten to pick up cutlery, he moved backwards, leaning over the person following him, apologizing as he did so.

The impatience in my mind dialled up a few notches but to some degree this went unnoticed in my awareness. I was more focused on the object (always a mistake): what was this guy doing? Wasn't he aware that he was in a queue and others were waiting behind him? What sort of person was he – bumbling around and obviously not very aware!

At this point, there was enough agitation in my mind for the habit of being with the mind rather than the object to kick back in. I noticed the strong judgements about this person from just 30 seconds' observation. I'd already decided what sort of person he was (unmindful and dawdling). Next, I noticed the craving in the mind and how it felt thwarted by his slowness. I realized craving was colouring how I saw this person and affecting how I interpreted his actions.

In that moment, it was very clear that I was noticing not the desired thing or outcome (fast-moving queue to a tasty lunch), which the mind usually experiences as very pleasant, but the ugly pole of *lobha* (wanting or craving).

Generally, we tend to hang out at the pleasant end of 'wanting', experiencing the seductive promise of the desired thing, whether a person, a taste, or sight or smell. We rarely look behind the scenes at what the mind in craving or aversion (its flip side) feels like and how it acts.

My thought in the moment of seeing the *lobha* mind strategizing, manipulating, pushing, making another wrong in order to get what it wanted, was 'how ugly is this mind, this process'. There was no judgement in this thought, simply that craving was unmasked and seen for what it was.

There is a Dharma List called the Viparyāsas. This is generally translated into English as the 'Topsy Turvies'! When something is topsy-turvy it's upside down and this is how the Buddha said we generally experience our world. We fail to understand the true nature of our ourselves and everything around us. We see what is impermanent as permanent, what is insubstantial as substantial; what we believe to be the causes of happiness are what will lead to suffering.

There is one more topsy-turvy, and here we usually mistake what is ugly and call it beautiful. We make our desires synonymous with what's beautiful and blow the pleasant aspects of sense objects out of proportion. In doing this, we fail to see the darker side of the mind that is going all out to get what it wants for itself.

It was satisfying to have seen craving for what it is. Some wisdom in the mind immediately let go of the impatience and desire to be at the front of the queue. It was fascinated with this new view.

It takes wisdom in the moment to recognize the true face of *lobha*. And it's not pretty!

Aversion (*Dosa*)

We are hard-wired for pleasure. In evolutionary terms, pleasure meant survival. The bitter-tasting berries more likely than not would have killed us, the sweet ones filled our bellies and gave us vital energy. But, as is obvious, the berry-eating hunter-gatherer's life was not all about pleasure and neither is ours today. It is inevitable that we have a mixture of pleasant and unpleasant experiences. In the twenty-first century in the West, this is something we often find unacceptable and that non-acceptance rears its head when the deal falls off the table, our holiday company goes bust, or our own body protests with its aches and pains.

All too often we react to even the small losses as if they should not have happened. There's the bakery that runs out of our favourite bagel or the friend who stands us up at the last minute. Even the weather frequently falls down in our estimation of what it should be! The cycle of suffering comes around again and again. We have amnesia about the place of dis-ease and disappointment in our lives.

It's said that all our moments of things not going our way hit us hard because they remind us of the ultimate loss that none of us can avoid, that of our own death. The thing we most fear is completely inevitable, but we live our lives, for the most part, in denial that it will ever happen. We attempt to stave off what is ultimately unavoidable. Denial is our strategy; it might not work very well but until we have other options it is all we know how to do. In the face of something unpleasant we try to push it away and, if possible, replace it with something pleasant. This pushing away is *aversion*, *not wanting*. We maintain an idea of what 'should' be happening in the face of what is happening in our direct experience.

Aversion manifests in many ways and includes *anger*, *hatred*, *irritation*, *resentment*, *resistance*, *boredom*, *disappointment*, and *frustration*. *Grumpiness* and *grumbles*, *moaning*, and *judgements* about ourselves and others equally all feature. Any sort of *complaint* in the mind can be included under the heading of aversion, or 'not wanting'.

While it is understandable that we resist and dislike things, does it help us? What we often find when we employ any of the strategies above is that we suffer. We often find mind states like anger, frustration, and grumpiness unpleasant to experience.

The Buddha had a simile for this dynamic. He said, 'It is as if a person were to be shot with a dart, and then with another one.' The first dart stands for the actual pain or discomfort of an experience, but the second dart is all the mental suffering that accompanies it. In the Buddha's words, 'he worries, he grieves, he laments, beats his breast, weeps and is distraught'.

So instead of suffering from, for example, the continuous rain on your holiday, in addition you suffer from your own anger and disappointment. You suffer twice, and you suffer more than if you had been able to accept the rain and make the best of it with multi-coloured umbrellas!

Other Forms of Aversion

There are some emotions in the aversive group that might surprise us. They include feelings that we wouldn't necessarily consider harmful or aversive, like *grief*, *loss*, and *sadness*. We can have views that such emotions are actually good to feel, that we are 'in touch' with ourselves when we feel sadness or grief. We can think they are painful but good or right feelings. It is easy here to confuse what might be psychologically beneficial with a spiritual perspective. On a psychological level, it is helpful to know what we feel *whatever* we're feeling, but spiritually we are looking to see where we identify with what's happening, and then giving special importance to certain emotions. If we distinguish sadness as a good emotion, there will be others that we're labelling as 'bad' or wrong. Awareness does not side with particular mind states, it simply knows the feel of 'not wanting' in the mind and heart, and wisdom recognizes what follows on, whether it is suffering from unskilful states or happiness from the skilful ones.

What these emotions like sadness or disappointment have in common with the more obviously unskilful mind states like resentment or hatred is that they lack an acceptance of how things are. When we feel sadness, it is often a mixed experience. If we gently examine our hearts and minds, we might find that sadness is composed of a tenderness and sensitivity, but also a strong wish for things to be different to the way they are.

It's important to understand we are not denying what we're feeling or trying to replace it with another more 'positive' emotion. If we do this, we risk 'spiritual by-passing', where we repress a difficult or painful emotion or thought because it doesn't meet our expectations of how a spiritual practitioner should act. When we police ourselves like this, we're no longer aware of what is happening and we can be under the sway of aversion or 'not wanting'. Whether the experience is physical pain, sadness, or rage, the instruction remains the same: can I be with this with a wise, spacious, and kindly attitude of mind and heart?'

Working with Pain

One of the most obvious forms of *dukkha* is physical pain, and our most common response to pain is aversion. We don't want it; we think it shouldn't be there and we'll do what we can to get rid of it. And yet we can learn so much from observing our relationship to pain and discomfort.

Dr Paul Brand was a social missionary during the 1950s in a very poor community in India with high numbers of people suffering from leprosy. He wrote a book about his experiences called *Pain: The Gift Nobody Wants*.[3] We don't usually see pain as a gift, but it is a helpful perspective that can start to change how we think about these unwanted experiences of pain such as headaches, tooth sensitivity, or backache.

Pain is our warning system. It tells us that something is wrong – that we need to stop and take that stone out of our shoe rather than walk the next three miles on it. Even a very young child will instinctively draw back quickly after touching a hot pan or pricking his finger on something sharp. Pain can tell us when we are pushing ourselves too hard and helps us learn to distinguish a 'good' pain from a 'bad' pain: for example, the enjoyable 'pain' of a firm massage, or the muscle burn we get when we're building up physical fitness through exercise, as opposed to the sharp twinges of a torn ligament.

Part of our human package is to feel pain and discomfort. We feel pain, and we *need* to understand what pain feels like to keep us safe and assess the dangers around us. So, in this sense, pain is a gift. It isn't random; it's usually there for a reason and even though we might find it deeply unpleasant. It can protect us from injury and disease and also alert us to the presence of those things. It's not all bad! In fact, it's extremely useful to life to be able to feel pain.

Right View of *Dukkha*

The Buddha had plenty of radical things to say in relation to discomfort, ill health, and ageing. He was very clear that all these things are part of the human condition. We can't expect to have only pleasant, enjoyable, and satisfying experiences in life; there are bound to be those that we experience as unpleasant, unwanted, and downright horrible. It can feel deeply counter-intuitive to relate to these painful experiences without aversion. We can fall into thinking that we're supposed to be feeling the opposite, and *like* the pain, and why on earth would you like having a backache?

The Buddha isn't saying we must like difficult or unpleasant experiences, but neither do we have to automatically react to them by mentally pushing them away, or physically contracting and tensing the body, trying not to experience pain. When we react like this, we stay locked into the experience, meeting aversion with more aversion. In meditation, we cultivate a different attitude where the open and spacious mind is not dependent on or reacting to the object (the pain) it is knowing.

I've been using the word 'pain' but it is important to remember to relate to our actual experience. 'Pain' is the label we generally give to physical sensations *that we don't like and don't want.* What we call pain is a concept and, while not denying the strength of the habit of our ideas about pain, we can start to remind ourselves of Right View in relation to this experience. Usually the concept of pain is coupled with aversion rather than Right View. Aversion or *dosa* will always regard pain as unwanted, whereas, to Right View, pain is just another object for it to be interested in.

Initially when we look at our direct experience, we might label these things as throbbing, pulsing, or stabbing. As we become able to stay with the experience with awareness, we might experience more of a sense of pressure, heat, or vibration.

Remember that we're prioritizing the growth of awareness, so if you notice strong resistance to the experience, don't try to be aware directly of the sensations for too long. A few minutes may well be plenty of time, otherwise the resistance and not wanting will keep growing and awareness will weaken. It's helpful to keep checking how you're relating to these particular sensations – as objects arising in experience, or some other relationship such as aversion or judging. If you notice aversion in the mind that is aware, let that become the object, and then you can also notice how you're relating to the pain. What is the aversion thinking? How does it manifest in the body? How is it feeling? Can you notice how knowing the aversion impacts on the sensations?

Journeying through Pain to Sensation

Since I was a child, I've regularly had very painful migraines. Like many people with migraine, I become acutely sensitive to bright light and loud sounds, so a dark quiet room is my refuge for at least part of every attack.

As I've had them from such a young age I had developed strong habits and attitudes as to how I dealt with them by the time I started to learn to meditate. As a child, I didn't want to miss out on exciting stuff so I would push through and carry on despite the pain I was in.

In my twenties, the habitual mind-set was one of frustration. Event after event was 'spoiled' through the pain overwhelming me. When I started meditating, I brought the same attitude to practice: I saw the pain as getting in the way and preventing me practising properly. This affected my confidence in my ability to meditate and kept in place a cycle of trying too hard, which led to frustration and then giving up!

For a long time, I was completely identified with the frustration and aversion. Each time I meditated with significant pain, I reinforced the habit of aversion.

Eventually I learned to meditate with more receptivity, and because the awareness was more important than any particular object, I relaxed somewhat. I could simply be aware. When I had a migraine, pain became my object. Just sitting during those times allowed me to be with powerful sensations. And when pain wasn't being pushed to the side to focus on the breath or some other object, there was some relief. This is simple. This is all I need to do right now. I can just be aware of what's happening.

Even though the pain remained, to quite a large degree, the frustration lessened. I started to notice other, more muted mind states of apathy and resignation (I called this 'not again mind'!) in relation to the pain. Of course, it is natural that strong pain has its effects; I would feel more tired, and I had to spend more time resting and in an environment that was soothing rather than stimulating. But I had a suspicion that there was more I could learn through this practice of receptive awareness and wise attention.

As I became more skilled in watching my mind – and through the mind, the sensations – various questions arose. These were not questions that demanded an answer but came from the quality of interest and wisdom in the mind. How was I relating to what was happening in the body? What sort of mental attitudes was I harbouring? Was there some sort of relationship between the mind and body that kept the pain going? These were all live questions that informed my meditation. One question came up repeatedly, investigating how I felt about the pain: 'When there is pain, to what extent is the mind joining in with the pain?'

Potential of the Independent Mind

Whenever I had a migraine, the awareness would go back and forth between the mind and the pain, looking simply to recognize what was happening in each arena. At first, and especially when the sensations were strong, I could barely tell the difference; there was just a flare of painful body and mind stuck together. But over time I could clearly feel the aversion, frustration, or stoicism in the mind, and notice that this was different from the hot, or stabbing, or pressing sensations.

This was to be celebrated; I was seeing where the mind was indeed joining in. I was able to recognize these mind states *from the perspective of awareness* rather than from being identified with the aversion.

Sometimes, aversion manifested as a sort of collapse where the mind had given up, which I could feel in the body. At other times, I might notice only brief feelings coupled with images – for example, of being able to be out in the sunshine without my eyes hurting. These moments would reveal that I wanted this experience to go away; I wanted things to be different to how they were.

From this point on, there were also times when awareness was simply able to notice pain as sensation – sometimes intense sensations and sometimes mild but simply happening in awareness. The benign quality of awareness was unhooked from what was happening in the body. Awareness was mindful of processes happening in the body without joining in, so the mind could be light and happy without the need for the object to change or go away.

The 'pain' sensations in those moments had truly become a Dharma object whose purpose and usefulness was to help grow awareness.

Craving and Aversion Are Opportunities for Awareness to Grow

When craving or aversion are in the mind and we're not aware of them, we retain our belief that whatever we want or don't want matters. We implicitly believe that the greed and aversion matter and so we tend to give in to our desires – having the new dress or the good meditation, or getting rid of troublesome thoughts when we sit, or the extra 5 lbs we gained on holiday.

And if we manage to have what we want or make what we don't want go away, the mind may well calm down, to some degree, and for some time. What is problematic with this scenario is that it is temporary and partial; the desire or aversion doesn't really go away but looks for the next thing it can want, and therefore there is still some degree of dis-ease. At the back of the mind, we're working to try and keep a stasis, trying to control conditions to remain favourable to our wants and desires. In this way, we're constantly 'managing' *dukkha* by feeding the beast's hunger with scraps.

But when we are willing to *stay with* whatever arises from greed or aversion, and not immediately act them out, we find awareness is present in that moment. Something new happens when we pay more attention to awareness and make an object from each experience. Over time, awareness becomes stronger and can be with even powerful physical discomfort and strong longing without strain.

A sense of freedom can arise when we start to see through our addiction to following these destructive forces of mind. A few victories are enough to increase our faith and enthusiasm, which in turn further boost curiosity, awareness, and wisdom. Although there will be many ups and downs, we never lose the taste of those moments of independence from objects, and intimations of a larger freedom.

Mindful Pause: Exploring *Dukkha* and *Dosa*

In this exercise, simply be aware of any time you notice something unpleasant in your experience. It might be as simple as waking up to stiffness in the body in the morning. Or being aware that you're feeling too hot or too cold. Don't automatically shift your position or change your clothing but 'stay with' what's happening. You are recognizing *dukkha* nature. This is not a problem. It is something the mind can be aware of.

Whenever you remember, recognize the sensations connected with what is happening. Is the body finding the experience unpleasant? Or is it the mind? Where is the *dukkha* experienced? Be aware of the stiffness or coldness and the mind that is finding it unpleasant.

To help the mind further tune in to this area of *dukkha*, you might choose a time frame of say 30 minutes. You can do this during sitting meditation or anyplace you can sit quietly.

Be aware whenever there is something the mind finds unpleasant and remind yourself this is an object arising in experience; it's not personal, it has arisen in dependence on causes and conditions.

You can just recognize how the mind is feeling, without going into a story about it. For example, and without judgement, you might notice irritation, low mood, or sadness.

Be aware of the relationship between the object and the mind. Can awareness recognize aversion in the mind? What does aversion feel like in the body and mind?

Check every now and again if some of the qualities of awareness are present in the mind. How do those qualities of calm, presence, and receptive effort affect the object?

Chapter six

A Universe Within
Working with Thoughts

> This subtle level thinking, this internal dialogue is what
> we are. It's how we function. We do everything because
> our internal dialogue tells us to do it. Even if it's to wait
> to see where the awareness will go, it's all directed but
> you don't see it. You think it did it by itself, that it's
> right there at the back of your head running the show,
> directing everything. That is the subtle level of thinking.
> But we are not used to turning back and recognizing that
> this is directing, and those are thoughts. In that internal
> dialogue is all our motivation.[1]

In this chapter we'll look at how we can become aware of one facet of
mind, that of the thinking faculty. We'll look in two main ways: first,
at how the thinking faculty so easily becomes dominant in the mind,
and ways to work with that; and second, at thinking as a process,
pointing us to look directly at the nature of a thought.

In some Buddhist traditions 'mind' is used as shorthand to indicate
mental activity and, in particular, thinking. In early Buddhism,
thinking, although part of mind, tends to be distinguished from mind
in general. Thinking is seen as just one mental faculty among many
that helps us construct and navigate our way through our world.
Although the thoughts and images in the mind are just a part of the
mind, they are a huge part of creating an illusory world, blinding us
to what is actually happening.

Through our minds, we create our world when many different
functions blend together into a seamless and convincing whole. We

reinforce this conviction every time we take our sense experience to be solid and real rather than momentary and ephemeral. This happens more easily when we pay more attention to *what* we see, hear, or touch rather than investigating *how* it happens.

While we continue to look outwards to seek meaning from our fleeting sense contacts, we will always miss what is most significant. In meditation, we make that counter-intuitive move to look inwards at what we call 'mind' to see for ourselves how it all happens. Without that inward-looking gesture, we're always just skimming the surface of our experience. Looking superficially and in the wrong direction, how can we hope to really understand ourselves and our world?

When we are looking externally it invariably means we aren't aware of *how* we are relating to our experience and we overlook just how involved we are with the *contents* of the mind. Despite the nebulous quality of the mind we can feel it directly, but getting lost in thinking obscures what we can learn. In order to recognize the mind more clearly, it can be helpful to identify its discrete functions such as thinking, imagining, remembering, or anticipating. The mind works in all these different ways and more. When we are aware, when we perceive things, or when we make decisions – all these processes happen in the mind. When we are aware of any of these mental functions or processes then we can say we're aware of the mind.

More than any other function, we associate the mind with our ability to think. We usually identify our thoughts with who we are. They are 'my' thoughts. 'I'm thinking.' We can verbalize our thoughts, but if we choose not to, they remain a private and personal part of our inner world. We can communicate our thoughts through spoken or written language, or we can have a complete and silent conversation with ourselves.

It is important that we learn to bring awareness to the mental process of thinking. When we do this, we have more understanding of how we talk to ourselves and we gain access to some of the views we hold. We also learn much from applying the Right View perspective to our thoughts. When we are able to see a thought simply as a thought arising in the mind there is the potential for deep insight into the nature of *anattā* (not self). Who or what is thinking this thought if not me?

Creating Our World

> Thought can organise the world so well that you are no
> longer able to see it.[2]

We probably give little thought to how much of what we take to be the reality of our external sense world is produced, manufactured, and constructed in our minds. We take information in through our senses from the sights, sounds, and tactile sensations around us, and they all blend with and impact on existing patterns in the mind: patterns of thinking, of perceiving, and of remembering, to name just a few. Threads of experience are constantly woven to renew and reinforce a sense of who I am.

Scientists have studied the phenomena of thinking and discovered that many of the thoughts we have, we've already thought before – perhaps as many as seventy per cent. Many of these will arise in the mind multiple times. We really do like repeating ourselves! Think of the number of times the same thought or very similar thoughts about a single topic have arisen in your mind.

Perhaps you can remember a journey you undertook where you felt slightly anxious. Perhaps your train had a tight connection and a repeated image appeared in your mind: you are running for the next train, loaded down with heavy luggage. There is a sense of being rushed and under pressure and various 'what if' kind of thoughts. These repetitive thoughts and images, regardless of whether they are accurate, are a part of the process of unconscious reinforcement of our ideas about who we are and how the world is.

A large part of how we create our world is through our thoughts, whether we speak them out loud or they remain part of our silent inner musings. We are in an almost continual dialogue with ourselves through our directed and intentional thoughts, our imaginations, our rehearsed conversations with others, and our nocturnal and daydreams. Some thoughts are obvious and we can recall them quite easily while others are much more subtle.

The type of inner thoughts we have and the *way* we speak to ourselves determines our inner topography. Eventually, this will spill over into our life. If we habitually speak to ourselves with irritation or judgement, constantly finding ourselves coming up short, this will manifest in some way. Perhaps our physical posture becomes a little resigned and slumped as if we're regularly fending off blows – which in a way we are. Emotionally, we might become a bit defensive as if how we speak to ourselves informs how we've come to expect others to speak to us. No doubt some of them will confirm our expectations and others may become unduly solicitous, privately thinking us over-sensitive.

Storytelling Mind

Most of us love a good story. Whether reading a novel or glued to a blockbuster movie or an addictive box set, we enjoy getting lost in a world that is not our own. We respond instinctively to a strong image, great prose, or subtle characterization. It feeds something in our psyche. The power of a simple phrase can conjure up a whole inner world or move us unexpectedly to tears or rage.

In September 2019 the student activist Greta Thunberg addressed the United Nations. The conference she was speaking at was televised internationally, so the whole world heard her use the phrase 'I have a dream'. Those simple words from a sixteen-year-old girl became words of incredible power as she evoked the passion, courage, and charisma of Martin Luther King, along with the values of liberty and justice at the heart of the American civil rights movement over sixty years ago. In four words, she linked all those strong feelings and values with the urgent need to act now against climate change and global warming.

Words and stories last through time and summon up a world. I've grown up with the words 'Ask not what your country can do for you, but what you can do for your country' embedded in my mind. For some reason, I strongly associated them not with John F. Kennedy's inaugural speech but with Winston Churchill and a powerful call to arms during the Second World War. It's only while checking my facts for this book I've discovered my error. Stories have power – for good and for ill – but they are not always true!

Our thoughts help to create the narrative to our lives. Sometimes the narrative or story is a good one and we like it. It's positive and full of possibilities; we feel pretty satisfied with it. Perhaps it is the story of a life where generally things go well for us and, on the whole, we act well within it, especially to those people who are important to us. Sometimes the story is full of woe and difficulty and we struggle with the *dukkha* in our lives. The storyline might be one of regret, of 'what I could be if things were different', and this influences how we feel about our life.

Although we might tend to incline one way or the other, usually we have both pleasant and unpleasant narratives over the course of our lives, even over the course of a single hour. What I'm calling 'the story' is how we think, often quite unconsciously, about our lives – whether good or bad things have happened to us. It is the raw data of experience interpreted and expressed through language: the story we tell ourselves.

Thoughts, of course, don't create a story alone. In the delicate and complex territory of the mind there are always several active players in any moment. A story is a potent mix of thoughts and images in the mind, but also feelings that are pleasant or unpleasant and many that are neutral enough to go unnoticed. Numerous sensations in the body – a fluttering in the chest, heat in the belly, pressure in the head or neck, the slowness or quickness of the breath – all play their part. Together, a combination of these elements can bring about the arising of emotions that drive yet more thoughts spilling over into speech and behaviour.

A crucial factor in the thinking process is a wonderful Pali word, *papañca*, which means proliferation. I touched on this in chapter 1 in relation to the mind that 'thinks about' rather than stays with the direct experience. It is even more relevant when talking about the storytelling mind. What proliferates is thinking itself, over-spilling like a waterfall, into a torrent of thoughts, images, and ideas. The raw data of our sense experience is drenched and drowned (out) in the process.

What starts off as a tiny stream of thoughts becomes stronger and more powerful. The thoughts and images are reimagined and reinterpreted through repeated unconscious riffing on them, like a jazz saxophonist improvising her way through a set. It is the nature of the mind to think, and there's nothing wrong or faulty with this, but when thinking proliferates and entwines with strong emotions, it is very difficult to remain aware; we are likely to be drawn into and become lost in the drama of the content.

Sometimes the worst that can happen is that the mind wastes a lot of time free associating when we want to be meditating. Many hours can be whiled away with the mind taking up and putting down ideas, moving from one to another, barely noticing leaps from one topic to another through a tiny link. Our reveries, pleasant though they may feel, are a spiritual dead end. They take us away from our experience in the present moment, and away from awareness. We can sometimes be astonished at how it has happened – 'How on earth did I end up thinking about *that*?'

It is when we fixate our thinking on painful or difficult happenings that the tendency of the mind to proliferate can really get into trouble. We get sucked into the content of the story and a vortex of thoughts of increasing intensity and volume can carry us to places of suffering and confusion in the mind. The more frequently this happens, the deeper the grooves of habit are worn in our mental make-up. It can be a very strange feeling when we wake up from a powerful story and we realize that our inner journey into a nightmare bears no relationship to the reality.

It is not for nothing that this phrase attributed to Mark Twain is so frequently (mis) quoted: 'Some of the worst things in my life never happened.'[3] There is a seductive quality to thinking which we find hard to resist – it is the 'all about me' factor. Thoughts act as the central piece revolving around the star of the show, which of course is me! It is what *I* think or don't think, *my* views, ideas, and opinions, what's important to *me*. Our thoughts reinforce a solid sense of self. Even when the thoughts are unpleasant, we gain security from relying on our thinking process to continue to reassure us of who we are.

When thoughts interact with feelings and body sensations the combination fuels an emotional reaction. Without awareness, a few thoughts can be conditioned by a passing feeling of low mood, and before you know it the mood has deepened into a more fixed mood of depression. Further thoughts such as 'I'll never get out of this' dig a deeper hole for the mood and a vicious cycle spins more thoughts and other emotions into it – a perfect descent into hell!

We create our own hells when our thoughts run riot, as well as our own temporary heavens. But in every moment, there is the potential to recognize whatever is happening, and to know it more objectively. Even with a jumbled, confused, and conflicted mind we can become aware of both the whole thing – conflicted mind – and the individual components of thoughts, feelings, judgements, and so on. Each moment of clear recognition can bring us a mind and body with a little less agitation and a little more peacefulness. Once we get a taste for peace, we become much more motivated to try to keep our awareness going.

Labelling Thoughts – A Provisional Strategy

We all have multiple storylines playing out by the dozen every day in our minds about ourselves and others we meet or think about. We are (or they are) the clever person with good ideas at work, the lazy slob who can't be bothered to do that boring task, the good meditator who sits every morning, the bad meditator (we can find any number of reasons here), the guilty practitioner who gets irritated, the greedy one who takes more biscuits with morning coffee, the lover, the anxious parent – the list goes on.

To start to get a handle on the storytelling mind it can be very helpful to objectify the type of thoughts we are having. We don't need to do this for long but, as a temporary measure, to become more aware of some of the patterns in the mind, we can use the technique of labelling. In any given moment, we sum up what the thinking mind is doing from the perspective of awareness and Right View. The simple practice of giving a soft mental label to the types of thoughts we have prevents the stories becoming too entrenched. We start to get to know the mind in a slightly new way. It can be as simple as labelling 'thinking' whenever you notice thoughts happening.

When we label thoughts or emotions, we are not trying to stop them happening or to make them go away. Labelling is simply a tool that helps us learn to recognize what is happening. We apply the principle that we're less interested in the *content* of what is happening than in the *process* of observing the experience – in this case, thinking.

Examining our thoughts can start to change the relationship from one where we are tightly bound to our thoughts to a more spacious one, within which we learn to notice what type of thoughts they are. Do they conduce to our own happiness and well-being? Are they contributing to lowering our mood or setting up an adversarial relationship to others? With a soft, curious awareness, we see when the way we are thinking leads to the clear seeing of wisdom or to furthering the agenda of the 'poisons' of craving, aversion, and delusion.

Thoughts can have a lot of momentum, especially when fuelled by unseen emotions, and so it can be difficult to create distance from them. It becomes very hard not to believe in the story, and unwittingly the sense of self becomes stronger through this belief, and from identifying with the thoughts as 'me' the thinker. We become more and more involved in a story about what's happening, and the label can be a way to reorient in the present and connect back with our direct experience.

Labelling works by recognizing different *types* of mental activity; we're summing up what is happening in the moment without getting overly involved with it. You might label 'planning' or 'anticipating' when you notice you're leaning into something that's going to be happening in the future. If you notice you're mentally caught up in something from the past, you could label it 'remembering'.

Other types of labels are 'judging', to catch the thoughts that deem your experience not up to scratch, or when you notice you're judging someone else. 'Comparing' mind is very helpful in catching insidious thoughts that compare the present moment experience with yesterday, or five minutes ago, or with someone else's experience which we might imagine is better or preferable to our own.

What labelling often does is make us more aware of some of the mental factors influencing the observing mind. It gives us some mental freedom to go from being completely involved with a thought and a big story to knowing 'ah, it's simply a memory'. We start to become more objective about our thoughts, and the small amount of distance from complete involvement in our thoughts can be powerfully freeing. It is the freedom of Right View in action.

Mindful Pause: Labelling Thoughts

When you are next meditating, or just sitting quietly and you feel fairly grounded in your body, spend some time noticing your thoughts. It is worth keeping the periods of watching the mind and watching thoughts quite short initially.

In between times, let your awareness register objects through the physical senses.

Initially, you might use the very simple mental label of 'thinking' whenever you notice thoughts in the mind. You just drop this silent label in lightly. You're not trying to catch every thought, especially if there are lots of them. Just drop in 'thinking' when you remember.

If you find that the thought stops dead when you notice and label it, check to see if you're using more energy than is needed. Remind yourself that you're looking to notice rather than stop or remove the thoughts and see if you can back off a little. Subtle objects require a subtle awareness and are easily hampered by a more forceful or energetic noticing.

Keep the awareness and the label light and playful. The label is not the most important part of the experience, but using it can help highlight the direct experience.

It's important that the label describes the type of thinking and helps objectify what's happening in the mind, rather than personalizing the content, making it more likely we'll get lost in it:

- planning
- anticipating
- remembering
- seeing (internal images)
- hearing (internal conversations)

- rehearsing (often when we're a bit nervous about an upcoming conversation such as a meditation review on retreat)
- repeating
- judging (in the sense of condemning rather than evaluating)
- comparing (to others, or to yourself on a previous occasion)
- wanting (any expression of craving or desire for sense pleasure)
- not wanting (any expression of aversion)

You can also label emotions simply to be clearer about what's happening in your experience. For example, when you identify 'sadness' or 'disappointment' and give it a label you can then stay with the feeling more directly, noticing how it feels in the body, and what sort of thoughts the mind has when sadness is present.

If you find that you're frequently carried off by your thoughts into stories and unawareness, you can return for a while to a more tangible object such as different body sensations or the sensations of the breath. Once there is a little more stability of attention you can open to thoughts again.

The Power of Thinking

One of the scary things in mental illnesses like depression is the thoughts that we have. In depression, there are often many thoughts that are self-denigrating and that focus on all that we find negative or difficult in our lives. Thoughts like 'I'm no good and my life is awful' or 'I'm useless, no one cares about me' reinforce feelings of self-hatred and low mood in an endless descending spiral. And, while with illnesses like depression we may well need the support of medication or talking therapy, the low mood and negative thoughts are something most of us are visited by, at least from time to time. The 'lens' that we're looking through in these moments is strongly aversive and full of hopelessness, producing dark thoughts. Without Right View, which enables us to recognize thoughts as simply thoughts, we are likely to believe the thoughts to be true.

A few years ago, I took some medication for the migraines I suffer from. One of the listed side effects was a small chance of 'unusual' thoughts or sudden changes of mood. Within a couple of months of taking the tablets I found myself having the very clear thought 'Oh well, if things don't work out, I can always kill myself.' I was quite shaken by the thought as my life was pretty good at the time. Although there were some major uncertainties ahead (I had left a job I found stressful and was starting a series of longer retreats), I was excited about my life and the possibilities opening up.

Further thoughts followed. In my room in the retreat centre in Myanmar was a rail running about 8 feet from the ground, from one wall to another. Almost idly, I found myself wondering if the rail would hold my weight if I tried to hang myself from it. The thought was clear and distinct but neutral in tone. It was also somewhat detached from my mood, which until the moment of the thought had been quietly buoyant.

Even though I knew the thoughts were a direct result of taking the medication, and from that perspective I was fascinated, they also frightened me. I was aware of the thoughts and I didn't quite believe them, but I was still worried that they might overwhelm me and I'd act on them. At times, I had some perspective, and at others, I was still identifying with the thoughts and believing them.

It felt a little bit like when you're looking down from a high cliff and feel the impulse to jump off, just to relieve the tension and discomfort of the fear of falling. Quite quickly, I decided to reduce the dose of the medicine I was taking and eventually stopped it completely. Within a week or so, the thoughts had gone.

We give a huge amount of power to our thoughts, but they are simply arising based on certain conditions; in my case, the cause was complex chemicals designed to calm down the pain signals in my brain. Without the ability to stand back and be aware of our thoughts we usually find ourselves unable to look at a situation from a more benign, kindly, and objective perspective.

When we are not able to step back from our thoughts, we give them enormous power – power that can claim our lives, or dictate how we feel about ourselves, or even bring one country to war with another. Understanding this, we can start to see the tremendous value in cultivating a new way of relating to thoughts.

When we notice the tendency to take particular thoughts very seriously, it can be helpful to remember the words of the Burmese teacher, Sayadaw U Pandita, when he says, 'Any thought can arise in any mind at any time.'[4]

We don't need to take thoughts so personally. They are conditioned by past habits. We can just let them arise and pass away. Through meditation we can start to take back that power, not through force, but through the power of mindfulness and clear seeing. In the following chapter we'll look at how we can also harness the power of thinking as a tool and a support to Right View and wisdom.

Thoughts Are Not the Enemy

Despite what I've written above, it is important we don't cultivate a relationship to thoughts that is based on fear or aversion, just as we don't want to be fooled into always going along with thoughts that confirm a pleasant emotional bias in the mind. We still need the all-important qualities of receptivity and friendly awareness to avoid opposing thoughts or buying into them. We are cultivating a quality of awareness that recognizes thinking as no more or less than any other happening in the mind.

Often the (unconscious) aim in our meditation is for the mind to be empty and free from thoughts. When we have this idea in the mind, we set up an inner conflict where the presence or absence of thoughts is a measure of failure or success in the practice. When we don't recognize this initial idea, each thought that arises in formal meditation will be unwanted, and the mind is primed to react with 'not wanting' every time it catches itself thinking. This turns the presence of thoughts, which in themselves are quite neutral objects, into a kind of tyranny to the mind.

It is helpful to clearly emphasize to yourself that it is not necessary to banish thoughts in meditation. This is the case whatever meditation practice you're doing but is particularly the case in more receptive-type practice where we are observing *whatever* is happening. We can make a distinction between being *lost* in thoughts and being able to *be aware* of the thinking that is happening.

We are aiming for the latter and to do less of the former, while understanding that *everybody* gets lost in thoughts! This happens repeatedly, for many, many years of meditation practice. Thinking is universal to all minds, it is completely essential to a human life, and it is a natural function of the mind. We've been getting lost in thoughts for longer than we've been able to speak, so we need to be patient to support awareness doing its job of simply knowing. In this way, we allow the habit to slowly unravel.

Do You Believe Your Thoughts?

In a very real way, our thoughts determine who we are and what we are capable of. This is partly because we tend to believe our thoughts. It is 'me' thinking them, so by implication, what I'm thinking must be true. All too often we don't question what our thoughts tell us – even when they are quite contradictory and we are convinced by one course of action only to be just as convinced five minutes later by its opposite. We believe our thoughts because we identify them as 'me'.

Our thoughts are completely entangled with the belief that I am the thinker of my thoughts. Even when we recognize our inconsistencies, it is still 'me' being inconsistent!

Once, during a meditation interview (where a student will talk about their practice to me), I could see that the person was getting quite tied up with the contents of his thoughts. He was giving a lot of significance to the storyline. I asked him whether he believed his thoughts. He paused to reflect and then said he didn't know, and we carried on talking. Two days later he came back for another interview and it was clear he'd taken my question very seriously. This student had watched his mind and come to a point of clarity. Yes, he said, he believed his thoughts.

We agreed that he would continue to notice thoughts as they arose, simply knowing a thought as a thought and not looking to go into the contents, although the contents would automatically be known to some degree. Towards the end of the retreat we met again. He had noticed many thoughts, he said, and most of them were complete nonsense. His thoughts were full of opinions and judgements often based on very little information. Or they looked to the future and wondered and speculated for quite extended periods of time. It was very hard to take the thoughts seriously. This was something of a revelation for this diligent student who had a lot of confidence in the rationality of his own mind. He discovered that when he became aware of his thoughts it was not wise to automatically believe them!

This type of investigation is possible because awareness and Right View are present. With Right View, we are practising to know a thought simply as a thought arising in the mind. It is not necessarily the truth. Right View and awareness lend a different quality to how we usually experience objects, and this is particularly noticeable with thoughts. We usually have such a strong association with 'our thoughts are us' that knowing a thought for what it is, feeling the *nature* of a thought, highlights the absence of self-referencing. Every moment that we are aware of self-referencing or the absence of it is a drama-free moment imbued with a significance that, over time, we learn rest in.

My student was more able to notice whether his thoughts were truthful or accurate and whether they needed to be paid attention to. This was especially true of the thoughts that were informed by the pulls of craving and aversion; he was able to learn how they impacted on his mind. He saw that often a thought was about how he could try and get something to happen or something else to go away.

Greed will tend to overemphasize the pleasant aspects of our experience and downplay the negative impact. Craving for excitement and for others to have a certain view of you might lead you to take up skydiving, for example. But that craving will probably overlook the expense involved, the potential dangers, and the amount of time spent sitting around in the cold waiting for the cloud covering the drop zone to disperse. I speak from experience here!

Aversion will tend to do the opposite. We might know someone who is a perfectly reasonable human being, but we really don't like their loud voice or the fact that they talk with a mouth full of food. We give the thought 'I can't stand the sound of their voice' a lot of power. We allow our dislike of one trait to colour how we see them, perhaps even thinking we couldn't be friends with them.

Different Types of Thoughts

We have different types of thoughts based on different sorts of minds. Some minds are lively and active and think many thoughts and easily dance off into stories. Others are quieter and slower and may have fewer thoughts but find themselves easily lulled into dullness and sleep. Some minds incline towards concentration and others towards investigation. Through watching your mind, you can come to appreciate the characteristics of your own particular mind. But all minds will think to a greater or lesser degree, and how they think, the patterns of thinking, will be similar. With practice, you can identify the different qualities to thoughts as they appear in different ways. Here are some of the ways you might recognize thinking in the mind:

- *Strong intentional thinking*. You're almost thinking in capital letters or bold type or thinking out loud. This type of thinking has a deliberate quality to it and tends to be quite easy to follow. You might think about your practice in this sort of way or follow through a line of argument in an article you're reading.

- *Proliferating thoughts.* We looked at these types of thoughts earlier in the chapter. This is where the mind is spewing out thoughts that condition further thoughts, quickly jumping from one associated storyline to another topic. These thoughts can be pleasant and useful, allowing meaningful reflection and intuitive flow of creativity where the mind roams freely under the watchful eye of awareness. But when proliferating thoughts happen out of awareness, they are a means for the growth of the 'poisons'.

- *Wispy wandering thoughts.* They don't have a lot of energy or a strong emotional colouring but at a certain level in the mind you'll find they are always there, interacting with intentions and perceptions. They create a base level of movement and activity in our minds.

- *Power thoughts.* Sometimes, when awareness is quite strong and light, you might notice that the mind doesn't go through a more laborious thinking process. I'll find I've just thought a couple of words or there has been as little as a single image in the mind and a whole story is known. It is as if the story has been compressed into mental data that is recognized by a signature password. The mind might then unwind itself and think the story 'out loud' in a sort of long hand, but you know it's not necessary, the content is already known to the mind.

All these forms of mental activity – and many more – can be noticed and help us to understand how the mind is working.

What Is a Thought?

If we're able to look at our minds, with a relaxed, curious attention, what do we see? As we gain experience watching the mind, we might notice that the direct experience of thinking is not quite what we expected. How a thought feels in the mind is not a uniform thing;

thoughts can come in different strengths and flavours. We're not trying to 'see' thoughts, but more to feel into the process of *how we know we're thinking* and what is happening in that moment.

Remember how little effort is needed beyond simply being present. With a forceful or overenthusiastic effort, the mind loses the flexibility and enjoyment that comes from the soft and receptive attending necessary for knowing a subtle object. Watch out for the mind jumping on a thought like a cat catching a mouse. Rather, we can approach softly from sideways on, glimpsing out of the corner of the mind's eye.

When we are quietly engaged with noticing thoughts, we will probably see how they are not a single thing. We talk about a thought, as if its nature was of one thing, but the observation reveals a flotsam and jetsam of items like a child's treasure hoard collected from the beach. Seaweed and different types of shells and pebbles rub along with specks of sand of different colours, fishing nets and ropes, and bits of washed-up crustaceans.

Similarly, a 'thought' consists of many different elements. These include images in the mind, some quick and shimmering and others clear and vivid. There will be a word or two – probably not as many as you might expect, and perhaps an urge in the mind towards action. You may see how the mind uses its senses to talk to itself, drawing in sights and sounds from the world around you, shaping its internal and external narrative.

Seeing the breaking up of a thought, from something that seems so solid into something so fragmentary and insubstantial – and conversely, watching the mind put back together tiny elements into a whole forged by belief – can be fascinating. In this way, by observing thoughts in an open and fresh way, we can see the process of constructing and falling apart going on in each moment of experience.

Learning to See Through Our Identification with Thoughts

The 'reacting' mind is our responsibility. We see the gross level. We see someone come and call us a fool and we get angry, so we think that this person made me angry. But we don't see the subtle thought processes that go on; the identification with the self, the pride that doesn't want to be called a fool. That's what makes the mind angry, not the person calling you a fool.

So that is how the mind is responsible. The lack in the mind is the lack of understanding of its own processes. This is the fault that lies within the mind. We suffer because of our judgements, ideas and preconceptions. We suffer because of a lack of wisdom and an inability to think in the right way.[5]

Recognizing thinking as it happens in the mind helps undermine our belief in ourselves as the fixed and permanent entities our stories say we are. So much of our belief in a 'self' is tied up with identifying with thoughts as 'me' or 'mine', but when we can be with our direct experience, we begin to recognize a thought as *just a thought.* Reminding ourselves to bring Right View to bear on our experience of thinking helps establish the training perspective that eventually becomes a natural way for the mind to relate to thoughts.

Using awareness, we can recognize when we identify with our thoughts. Identification is the feeling or sense that 'I am' the thought or that the thought is 'mine'. Obviously, these are not necessarily conscious thoughts, or they would be easy to recognize. Identification is subtler and can often be noticed through a feeling of contraction or mental or physical tightness around any aspect of experience. There can almost be what I call a 'feeling of me' that we can learn to recognize.

Where we can usually see ownership and identification happening most strongly is in the moments where a belief (expressed through a thought) is challenged. When we have a difference of opinion with someone and we are identified with our thoughts and ideas, we will often feel threatened by the other person. A seemingly innocuous discussion can become quite charged, as though we're no longer talking about the issue at hand but something unspoken that has slipped into play. It is as if by challenging our ideas, our very self is threatened.

And this is exactly what is happening: if my ideas and thoughts are rejected or dismissed or ignored, 'I' am being rejected or ignored. If we don't recognize what is happening this can lead to painful states of upset, anger, and defensiveness. Even in its milder moments when we are not aware of taking ownership of thoughts, identification creates tightness and rigidity in the mind and body ('I am the sort of person who is like *this*', or 'why can't we do it the way *I* want?'), with none of the flexibility and openness of awareness and wisdom.

If awareness and Right View are active in the mind, we can start to catch the feeling of 'threat mind' and the suffering it brings along with it. We start to see the clinging and identification to things, some of which are relatively unimportant to us, and it is a relief when the mind recognizes the identification and lets go of them.

However, there are many issues of politics, social injustices, and health care that we don't want to let go of. They matter to us and are part of how we express our values. What is important in every case is that we recognize the role of thoughts in whipping up our identification with views and emotions and increasing painful clinging.

We don't want to let go of acting effectively in the world, but we will suffer more by acting out our rage, righteous indignation, or strong craving. When we act from a place in ourselves that is informed by awareness and wisdom, our actions will be more creative, more appropriate, and wiser. Practice will not diminish our effectiveness or desire for peaceful protest or passion for justice, but it will positively impact our actions through the state of mind we act from.

When there is momentum in practice, and awareness and Right View are consistently strong in the mind, we start to recognize thoughts in the same way we recognize a sensation in the body. We relate not to the concept and content of the thought or body part, or what we are hearing. When we know in our direct experience that a thought is just a thought stripped of all the accretions of self, we have a taste of the freedom that comes when the mind drops its identification with thoughts and rests with simple knowing.

Mindful Pause: Getting a Feel for When the Mind Is Identified with Experience

Check that awareness is present and how that feels in the mind and body.

Tune in every now and then to thinking. Practise distinguishing between the content of the thought, and how a thought feels in the mind.

How does identification or sense of ownership manifest? How can you feel it?

Notice any tightening or contraction in the body. Or sensations connected with emotions. Are these connected with a sense of self?

Can you notice when there is less identification with your thoughts? How does it feel to have positive distance from the thoughts, and be aware of thinking as a process?

You might want to label emotions arising alongside the thoughts.

Be aware of where you get 'caught' by thoughts and unreservedly believe the content.

Notice the emotional impact from believing the thought and stay with the feeling rather than the thoughts.

Mindful Pause: Practising Watching for the Sense of Self When You Are with Others

If you are with another person when strong identification with your thoughts arises, it can be helpful to try and take a bit of time alone to be with the reactions with some awareness, and to allow the mind time to calm down.

If this isn't possible, you can withdraw a little from the discussion (if there are more than two of you) so you can watch your mind. Or you can change the topic to something more neutral and continue to watch your mind.

Remember, you're not changing the object (the topic) to avoid the identification or the strong thought patterns and emotions that arise with it. You're recognizing that the mindfulness is not strong enough in that moment and is likely to be overwhelmed.

You give the mind a chance to build up its resources so that, when it is stronger, you can come back to observing how it is reacting to the object.

You are making space for a new kind of thinking.

In my early days of meditating, in the second half of the 1980s, I lived in east London close to where my teacher, Sangharakshita, lived and worked. He came across as a disciplined man; he wrote many books and would spend each morning at his desk. Both in person and when he gave lectures, his speech was slow and deliberate as if he was very clear what he wanted to say. I remember hearing a story about him where he was asked about something that needed some reply. His response was, 'I'll think about that next Thursday at 3pm.' This story gained mythic proportions over the years; to have such control over your thoughts was unheard of for most of the people I knew. I was in my early twenties and thoughts regularly popped out of my mouth without the benefit of any mental filtering, let alone deciding *when* I was going to think about them!

Actually, the filter still fails on occasion! But I have much more of an understanding these days of how to work with thoughts, and this includes deciding when to give a particular topic some mental space. It is not a mystical thing after all, but simply mindfulness. Thoughts will arise, of course, but to pursue them has become much more of a choice; is it the appropriate time and do I have all the information needed to think about a topic and come to a decision if required? The quality of *sampajāna*, or that which 'clearly knows' what is needed, does its job.

Being aware of our thoughts allows us to make wise choices. This might mean not allowing the mind to run down its familiar routes when you are trying to write a book, do your job properly, or not offend someone. Sayadaw U Tejaniya is fond of saying, 'The mind is not yours, but you are responsible for it.' He is emphasizing that although the nature of the mind is impersonal, we have some influence through training and encouraging it in a positive direction. When we give the mind something to do, such as be aware of thoughts, the thoughts are less likely to run amok.

As we learn to recognize thinking as it happens – not to make it stop, but to know its conditioned and self-less nature – we are less and less frequently led into unconscious story making. Awareness and wisdom do their jobs of knowing objects, and the world of thinking and imagining become yet more objects simply to be known. This naturally leads to more spaciousness in the mind as awareness has become more influential than other objects and its knowing quality becomes much clearer. The spaciousness is also the result of the afflictive emotions not having a chance to proliferate through the fertile ground of our thoughts, like weeds covering every available bit of soil.

A new kind of thinking can come about. It is governed more by wisdom, with awareness as its guardian. Wisdom thinks differently compared to a mind dominated by greed, aversion, and delusion. Wisdom thinks about what is best for the whole in any given situation. Wisdom is not governed by self-interest, but by a curiosity about practice, and a desire to explore and understand.

It takes a mind that is happy, relaxed, and interested to be present in this kind of way without forcing any sort of agenda. What is needed is a quality of awareness that sticks to nothing and rejects nothing but together with Right View sees more and more clearly.

Mindful Life Moment: Let What You Love Lead You to Wisdom

Tom Lubbock was the chief art critic for the *Independent* newspaper in the UK. He was known to many for his weekly column where for five years he wrote with brilliance and passion about a piece of art, usually a painting.

He died in 2011, at the age of 53, of a tumour that struck at the speech and language part of his brain. He made his living, and his life's meaning, from words, and it was to words he turned during the short years of his illness. Despite his treatment he continued to work, turning his intelligence and humour to his own predicament, producing a beautiful memoir.[6] As he gradually loses the ability to speak and even to form words into sentences in his mind, he movingly charts his inner experience, with every word hard won, and increasingly ungraspable, slipping through his fingers like water.

Naturally his investigation turns to his relationship with language. He writes about the 'mystery of summoning up words': 'Where are they in the mind, in the brain? They appear to be an agency from nowhere. They exist somewhere in our ground, or in our air. They come from an unknown darkness. From a place we don't normally think about.'

At first, he equates losing language, along with the understanding of speech and writing, with the loss of his mind: 'These losses will amount to the loss of my mind. I know what this feels like and it has no insides, no internal echo. Mind means talking to oneself. There wouldn't be any secret mind surviving in me.'

But, as he stays with the experiences that have piqued his lively curiosity, he later writes: 'I am faced practically and continually with a mystery that other people have no conception of, the mystery of the generation of speech. There is no command situation [in the mind], it goes back and back. Where the self lies at the heart of the utterance – the speaker generating the word – is always clouded.'

I think that Tom Lubbock here was hitting on the mystery of the nature of self, the lack of 'command central' or 'manager in charge'. He came up close to the obscured and cloudy inner view, expecting to see something that would confirm his sense of self-identity, and could not do so.

This is the territory we investigate with curiosity when we recognize thoughts as thoughts and start to see their ephemeral and intangible nature. What seem so powerful and influential arise and disappear in a moment if we don't hold on to them. Because of the damage to his brain it was more difficult for Tom to generate or hold on to thoughts, and so his experience was similar to that of the meditator. The sense that we are our thoughts can't hold up to the scrutiny of awareness and the power of interest.

As Tom's language decreased further, he noticed something more; as thoughts and language were disappearing, something that I would call awareness was still there. 'Knowing' or 'noticing', 'paying attention' and 'recognizing' were still on-line, and his experience was undiminished.

He writes: 'But I find my brain is still busy, moving, thinking. I am surprised. My language to describe things in the world is very small, limited. My thoughts when I look at the world are vast, limitless and normal, [the] same as they ever were. My experience of the world is not made less by lack of language but is essentially unchanged. This is curious!'

It is impossible to know exactly what someone else means through their words, but I resonate with Tom Lubbock's. His curiosity, courage, and good humour all allowed him to journey, exploring the nature of consciousness and its relationship to thoughts and language.

If we could bring even a little of this attitude to our own lives, who knows what would be possible in comprehending the nature of mind?

Chapter seven

Encouraging the Wisdom Mind

> One cannot speak of wisdom in terms of 'knowing' or of
> 'feeling'. It is both.[1]

Wisdom (*paññā*) can seem like one of those things that you've either
got or you haven't. It's perhaps easier to understand that mindfulness
or awareness can be cultivated, along with other qualities such as
compassion or concentration. Wisdom can seem a little different because
of its associations with the goal of practice and we can conclude that
therefore it must be a long way off. If you study Buddhism you get the
strong sense that there is a lot to practise and a lot to understand before
significant progress is made. After all, even someone as exceptional as
the Buddha took seven years as a wandering holy man before becoming
Awakened or Enlightened. And while it may be true that, on the whole,
deep and permanent insights depend on consistent and sincere practice
over time, wisdom may be more accessible than we think. Of course,
what is meant by wisdom or insight depends on how we define our
terms, which I'll do below.

For some people, wisdom comes in seismic shifts of deep and
significant understandings that redefine what we've thought to be
true and real. Insight may burst into our lives in meaningful and
sometimes disruptive ways, or it may be very simple and profound,
as in some of the stories of the Buddha's disciples.

However, for most people, becoming wise is a gradual process
marked by many momentary insightful understandings on different
levels. As the path unfolds over time you recognize that the mind
starts viewing things in different ways; you experience yourself as
kinder and more deeply in touch with your experience. There is an
image that describes this process beautifully.

Imagine a sheet of fabric like cotton or canvas, pinned vertical like a sail, with light, perhaps sunlight, shining behind it. The fabric is thick enough to block out most of the light so just a muted and shadowy colouring remains. With each moment of clearer seeing, a tiny rent appears in the cloth, each one separate from the others. As more tears appear, some join up, forming a larger hole that allows in some of the light behind. With time, whole areas of the cloth are torn and great shafts of light go through and beyond the fabric, illuminating everything in their path. Eventually, it is no longer possible to make out the cloth anymore and the light is completely unhindered, and nothing is hidden from it.

In this chapter, we'll look a little more at what's meant by 'wisdom' – and its opposite, delusion or ignorance – and how to recognize them both working in the mind.

Three Levels of Wisdom

The early Buddhist tradition talks of three levels of wisdom. This can be a very helpful teaching as it spells out what we're looking for and the different ways wisdom manifests. If we know about these three categories or levels, we are much more likely to be able to recognize the wisdom quality working in the mind. It may be 'little' wisdom, or it may be 'capital letters' wisdom, but that is less important than being able to recognize it for what it is, to be *aware* of it. We start to know how wisdom *feels* in the mind and body and this has the beneficial result of lifting our confidence and faith in ourselves and the practice, which stimulates an increasing desire to practise.

I will interpret this teaching of the three levels of wisdom mainly in the light of the meditative practice presented in this book, but its remit covers the whole of the Buddha's discourse.

The more the mind can recognize the wisdom faculty, the more future moments of wisdom are conditioned to arise. Our recognition strengthens the growth of clear seeing and non-reactive awareness; these two qualities reinforce each other, laying down the conditions for further understanding and freedom of mind and heart.

First Level of Wisdom

The first level of wisdom is primarily conceptual. It is what we hear or read about the Dharma and what we understand intellectually. We need to have some idea about what we are meant to be doing in meditation practice, and through hearing or reading the instructions we can follow them. We're able to listen to audio talks or a teacher or read a few paragraphs of a helpful text so we can keep remembering what we're meant to be doing in meditation. In this way, we are gradually able to recall relevant ideas and attitudes that help us practise. As I mentioned previously, U Tejaniya talks about this as 'borrowed wisdom'. It's not yet ours; we borrow it from outside until we have digested it and understood it for ourselves.

To support meditation practice, we study the Dharma to develop some understanding, in theory at least, of both the Buddha's teachings and the goal of Awakening. Our intellectual understanding of the teachings supports our ethics, meditation, and wisdom practice; we come to see what is meant by the teachings of the Buddha and how we apply them to our lives.

Sayadaw U Tejaniya talks about this as information gathering, and awareness practice as 'collecting data'. For some reason, although I'm not very tech savvy, I like the idea of data collection. It implies that awareness is working away in the background of the mind, and through practising well the mind is naturally gathering information.

Another image I like is of a jigsaw puzzle. You might have a few pieces in place with bits of blue sky in opposite corners and with no idea what the overall picture looks like, but you have the completed image on a cardboard box you can refer to! At a certain point, the two scenes start to resemble each other. The same is true with more and more moments of intellectual understanding; on a certain level, you are joining up the dots and seeing different connections in your overall understanding of the Dharma and in how you work with your mind.

Second Level of Wisdom

The second level of wisdom comes through practising with the 'data' the mind has collected and taken in. That might involve thinking about our practice, thinking about Dharma ideas and concepts, and reflecting on them. This is a valuable part of our learning and I give this a little more space later in this chapter. But the main point to stress at the moment is that the second level of wisdom is very much about recalling what we have learned so far from our reading and hearing Dharma talks or meditation instructions and applying that to our actual experience.

Sayadaw U Tejaniya calls this the 'intelligence' aspect of working in the practice. This is not intellectual intelligence but the ability to marry the receptive quality of mind with keeping the initiative in practice. We actively assess how the awareness is working in the mind, but in a very *receptive* way. If the mind is drifting or sleepy or regularly lost in thoughts, we recognize that these habits of mind aren't helpful to awareness. We're then able to draw on the information we know about how to practise (the first level of wisdom). The questions we've used in earlier chapters, such as 'what's happening now?' or 'what is the mind knowing?', are helpful in clarifying the mind state and seeing it more objectively.

Other questions then might arise, such as 'what's needed now'? or 'what would be helpful to do'? What out of the information gathered so far can I apply in this moment in practice? With the second level of wisdom we have the information and we are confident enough to experiment for ourselves.

It's important to keep the emphasis on receptivity. It might be that your 'strategy' for overcoming sleepiness is simply to be more mindful, to make a stronger intention to be present, and to be aware of what sleepiness feels like in your experience. But you have the wisdom to see when awareness is not enough, and when the more active strategies – keeping your eyes open or changing your posture from sitting to standing or walking – are necessary.

The insights come when we understand something in a slightly new way. Perhaps you are caught in a habitual mind state such as judgement or disappointment and it is creating a lot of mental and emotional suffering. You feel really stuck in it and the thoughts are firing off into intensely uncomfortable stories, but you continue to try to be aware of it and to know the stories and feelings for what they are. And at some point, there is a moment of experiencing all that feeling and thinking simply as the mind in conflict in that moment. Through continued awareness and wisdom there is a change in how you experience the moment. You find that you're taking that mind state much less personally – not because you're trying to, but because in that moment that is the perspective of the mind, the object is naturally seen in a new way.

As we apply the teachings we've heard and understood to our direct experience, we become more fluent in practice. We've internalized the instructions and can use our own experience to drop more deeply into the practice. We start to recognize what works, and what doesn't, to help awareness or receptivity or stability of mind grow stronger. As we become more self-guiding, the conceptualizing mind is less dominant and a subtler, more intuitive sensing takes over. In the second level of wisdom, awareness and Right View can work increasingly well at recognizing what is happening in experience in a more objective way.

We develop a clearer sense of 'knowing' what is needed, of what is beneficial to take the practice further, and we regularly have small but significant 'aha!' moments where we see something in a new and satisfying way. The 'aha!' moments are small openings into a different perspective on some aspect of our experience. A lot of the work of practice takes place in this second level of wisdom. If our practice is working well, we should experience these moments of significance quite regularly.

You could describe the difference between the first and second levels of wisdom through a driving metaphor. In the first level, we're learning the highway code and having some driving lessons. It's all quite unfamiliar territory but we take in the new information to help us learn this skill. Working with the second level of wisdom, our gear changes and mirror checks have become smooth and automatic. There is a sense of increasing mastery as we put our learning into practice. We know the rules of the road without having to think about them, we can anticipate hazards, and drive in difficult weather conditions. We're safe to be on the road!

It can really help to have the spirit of playfulness in your practice. When we play or experiment, we worry less about what's the 'right' thing to do and we are willing to try things out. This is very much part of that active intelligence. When I first learned to meditate, one of the things that was most unhelpful was that I tried to do what I was told for too long. I didn't have the confidence to deviate from the instructions even when it led to a lot of mental and physical tension. I was constantly referring to what I thought were the rules of the practice.

Understandably, when we first learn a practice we need to do it as we've been taught, but once you know the structure and have tried it out over a period of time, *assess how it is working for you.* This doesn't mean dropping the parts that you don't like, but do feel free to try out changes of posture or the type of effort you're using and how you do the practice. On retreats, I often tell students to choose whatever practice will best support awareness in that moment. This might turn out to be watching the breath or the mindfulness of breathing. We tune into ourselves and assess how the mind is, and what would be helpful. You might choose something that I have mentioned once in passing but for you it is really significant; or you might prefer meditating in the garden, if that's where you can clearly see awareness is working best.

Third Level of Wisdom

The third level of wisdom is insight (or wisdom) proper. We understand something of the nature of our experience clearly, deeply, and permanently. This understanding is not something we can control or will into being. We can't make insight happen. Yet, by diligently practising with the first two wisdoms, particularly the second, once we have a reasonable grasp on the teachings of the Buddha we are doing all that is necessary.

At some point, the moments of significance (aha! moments) lead to the more strongly transformative insights of the third level of wisdom. Part of the wonder of this process is that we train in something and put the conditions in place, but we don't know when the results will come. We need to let awareness and wisdom do their work and not worry about how many insights we're having or how big they are. It is best just to appreciate those moments when the mind is naturally seeing something in a new way. We can celebrate the freedom in the mind that is not clinging to objects and notice how that feels.

When these moments of direct intuition or a clear understanding of how things are come, they stimulate trust in the practice and greater enthusiasm to practise. There may be a temporary shift in perspective or a more long-term effect – in a sense, it doesn't matter; we just continue to practise. There might only be a subtle shift in perspective, but it can change everything in ways we could not have imagined beforehand. This is the insight or wisdom aspect.

So, we have *information*, *intelligence*, and *insight* as the three levels of wisdom. They are a dynamic interacting process; in any moment when we're aware with Right View the mind will be gathering data and using its intelligence to discern what is happening in experience. When it has enough understanding, more significant insights follow. Continuity of mindfulness, curiosity, and receptivity are all conditions that support the process.

The World of Delusion (*Moha*)

> If only delusion is present, conditioning is set, and such
> a person will act entirely according to that conditioning.
> If there is no interest in wisdom, the mind is just a push-
> button system that is triggered by external sources.
> Conditioning dictates all outcomes.[2]

We can learn to recognize *wisdom* when it is in the mind and its opposite, *delusion*, also known as *ignorance*. Ignorance is the third of the mental 'poisons', of which craving and aversion are the other two. We looked at these enormously influential states in chapter 5.

The Pali word for delusion is *moha*, which I particularly like as it conjures up images in my mind of fluffiness or fuzziness. It speaks of clouds hiding the clear blue sky from being seen, just as with a mind of delusion we can't see clearly what is going on. To me, the Pali word really conveys something of the meaning of this root cause of suffering. The nature of ignorance is to ignore and what *moha* does best is obscure the true nature of experience. What we are left with is something partial, selective, and unclear from which to try and make sense of ourselves and our world.

Some of the mental qualities that constitute ignorance and delusion are easily available to awareness if we know what we're looking for. When we see through the lens of Right View, we are able to see delusion from the perspective of wisdom. The effect is to dispel some of ignorance's distorting and misleading qualities. When delusion is seen more clearly, its negative influences are reduced and, to some degree, understood.

Because of this quality of obscuring what we can know directly, *moha* is the most difficult of the 'poisons' to recognize. It is the most pervasive and colourless. *Lobha* (greed) and *dosa* (aversion) add plenty of colour to the mix, with their splashes of fiery, bright emotions, dark moods, and big passions.

Delusion underpins the other two poisons and interrelates with them in different ways: whenever craving or aversion are in the mind then ignorance is also there. Delusion will always be misreading any situation according to a basic wrong view of a self that has some fixed and inherent nature. This wrong view arises from a fundamental misreading of experience which creates a duality in the mind, most commonly manifesting through what I want or don't want.

We can't separate craving (*lobha*) or aversion (*dosa*) from ignorance. The three poisons are different ways of expressing our basic delusiveness. This, of course, is not perversity on our part. We are doing our best to obtain happiness, and the only way we know how to do this is through trying to get pleasant and enjoyable things and trying to minimize what we find difficult or unpleasant.

The Buddha's teaching is quite counter-intuitive in the way it states that suffering comes through both grasping for pleasure and pushing away the unpleasant, and that the cessation of suffering is brought about through a clear experiential understanding of this dynamic. A new and surprisingly simple way of relating to experience is required to help facilitate this understanding.

Recognizing Delusion

It's important to remember that *moha* is simply another aspect of mind. There is nothing wrong with our practice if we spot it, and when we first use this particular label to notice different ways that delusion shows up, we're bound to see it quite a bit. It is important not to judge ourselves or try and get rid of it or make our observations (which are momentary) into a more permanent 'add-on' to our sense of self – 'Oh, I'm so full of ignorance!'

A basic equation is *more delusion = less wisdom* and *more wisdom = less delusion*. This equation is relevant until Awakening and so it is not surprising that delusion seems fairly ubiquitous! If you are noticing it quite frequently, this is a cause for celebration and not despondency. The more it is clearly known, the more you can learn about its effects on the mind and its actions and behaviours. Remember, the way Right View works is that if you are noticing delusion in the mind, then the awareness that is noticing it is not of the same (delusive) nature. To some degree, you will be observing with wisdom, with Right View, and this is enough.

As we've been doing all along, we can take *moha*, delusion, as an *object of experience*. We objectify it so that we observe its 'nature' and get to know how it functions in the mind. We can recognize how delusion affects the mind and know its characteristics through directly observing them. Rather than being in the midst of the clouds of *moha*, having no idea where we are, we learn to open our eyes, to describe what is surrounding us, and watch the cloud move on according to its own nature. We are then able to see its shape, colour, and insubstantial quality, as well as the blue sky all around it.

On one of my long retreats in Myanmar I learned to recognize *moha* and then found it popping up all over the place when watching my mind and in my speech and interactions with others. I saw different manifestations of delusion, many of which, though they were familiar mind states, I hadn't recognized as delusion before. I also had a lot of fun – which really helped me engage – in coming up with a job description for *moha* from what I'd noticed in my observations. I then contrasted *moha* with another job description, that of wisdom or *paññā*.

Delusion would often show up as tiredness at times when I knew I was well rested. The tiredness went along with feeling a bit bored and disengaged; interest in the practice would be quite low. The lack of motivation to change this state was another indication that *moha* was around. I would sometimes come back to present moment awareness in this slightly dull and apathetic state and think 'I don't know what to do'. Then would follow a fairly ineffectual period of wallowing in confusion. Over time I was able to maintain awareness to see more clearly how delusion was affecting my ability to think clearly from a Dharma perspective.

In documenting the ways in which *moha* played out in my mind, what was immediately clear was the obfuscating and wool-gathering aspect of delusion. Delusive thinking keeps us wavering and indecisive about a course of action – in fact, often, *any* course of action at all. *Moha* is a master at time wasting; it was fascinating and slightly horrifying to see how whole meditations could be frittered away through not quite getting down to it!

Even though 'getting down to it' simply means being present with Right View, rather than a more energetic doing of something, *moha* can still prevent effective engagement indefinitely. Delusion is countered by simple present moment awareness – but we need to *remember* to be aware. That small but crucial inner gesture makes all the difference.

It's helpful to recognize that *moha* isn't different from our usual habits and patterns, and that our normal mode is delusive. Whenever we're not acting out of wisdom we will be mired in delusion or ignorance. The goal in practice is to change the equation of our heart and mind so that, in any moment, we have more wisdom and less delusion.

Occupied but Not Engaged

Dharmachari Subhuti, when talking about 'just sitting' practice as a receptive and formless type of meditation, coined the phrase 'being occupied but not engaged'.[3] This beautifully describes a facet of the *moha* mind. Another way we could label this mind state in meditation might be *going through the motions* mind. We are doing something, but we're not especially interested or connected with it.

We might meet this mind at work with the routine tasks that form part of most jobs, or when we half watch TV while doing something else. Or it could be the state of our daily meditation. To paraphrase a line from one of my favourite films, *The Abyss*, 'we're doing it, but we ain't diggin' it!' This type of mind can become the habitual way we engage with our lives. On the surface, our lives can look full and productive, but all the activity can be a substitute for a deeper and more meaningful connection with ourselves and our practice. All too frequently we keep ourselves just occupied enough to keep the subtle dissatisfactions of life at bay.

Occasionally I catch myself when I'm reading and recognize that I'm not that engaged. I'm usually skimming the text and not fully interested in it. There can be a sense of filling up time before the next activity. This is usually before I go to sleep so, understandably, I'm tired or wanting to relax at this point, but even so it points to an unhelpful habit where it is easy to sleepwalk through life. Sometimes, when I recognize this, I'll choose another book I'm more interested in and that's usually a bit more demanding.

At other times, I'm curious enough about this tendency to take it as an opportunity to observe how *'moha* mind' feels. I switch more of my attention to watching the mind and how it is relating to the object. It is a real challenge to engage with each moment and not tune out in the ones we unconsciously judge to have little value.

Mindful Pause: Engaged Rather Than Occupied

While 'going through the motions' mind is something we can recognize in relation to any object at any moment, it can be especially helpful to notice it in relation to screen time.

Often our attention is only partially taken up by a game on our phone, or online research. We are doing it in an absent-minded sort of way, pulled along by the hooks designed to get us to click to yet another page. Keep checking to see what the quality of mind is like as you use any sort of technology.

When you notice that you're not really engaged – perhaps you're skim reading or flicking between your phone and the TV, for example – tune into that state of mind as you continue the activity. What does it feel like? What do you notice about the quality of your mind?

Keep reminding yourself to stay present and grounded, and let the awareness move between (seeing and hearing and touching) the screen activity and the mind.

What are the thoughts and feelings in the mind? How does the awareness feel?

In doing this you might find that the awareness you are bringing in naturally broadens out what you're aware of. You might notice your posture more, perhaps a bit hunched over your screen, and then your fingers on the keyboard, your feet on the ground.

Try stopping the activity for a few minutes and just watch the mind. Notice any compulsion to continue or pick up the phone – recognize craving working with *moha*.

If *moha* is strong, you might find it rallies the other poisons to its cause; there might be irritation at the exercise and you just want to get back to the screen.

Recognize the quality of the mind and see if it changes as awareness is prioritized. You might notice awareness brighten the mind so that it becomes clearer and more relaxed.

Whatever you do next, carry on in awareness.

Thinking about Your Practice

There is a further thing that can aid our path to wisdom and clarify what is happening in practice: we can *think about* our practice. This comes under the second level of wisdom. After formal sitting or walking meditation, take a couple of minutes to assess how your practice went. Use awareness and Right View in your assessment so that the quality of reflection is coloured by a kind and unbiased interest rather than a nit-picking perfectionism. In this way, you can start to understand the causes and conditions that contributed to more continuity of awareness or more being lost in a spiral of emotion. You will get more from your practice through looking at it in this way.

Sangharakshita was once asked by a student how someone could become wiser, and what they would need to do to have a practice more like their teacher. He replied: 'At the end of each day reflect on what has happened during that day.' It was not clear to me at the time I first heard this many years ago, but I'm convinced now that the unspoken and implicit attitude behind these words was, 'reflect in the light of what you know of the Dharma'.

It can be a powerful practice to take time to think about how you've practised that day. The value of reflecting on what has happened makes us more consciously aware of what went well in practice and what didn't. It is then possible to set up helpful conditions for the next time the same situation arises, whether that is a meditation where you lost your mindfulness or a personal meeting where you lost your temper!

You could consider reflections such as remembering where you lost mindfulness that day and what the result was. Did the lapse in awareness affect your ethical practice? How were your actions and speech affected? What were the effects when you felt quite aware; what was the quality of mind like? Where was wisdom at work in the mind? How aware were you of different qualities in the mind, such as delusion, compassion, irritation, or patience?

It sounds like such a simple thing to do, and I clearly see the value of it, and yet, although I've had periods where I've done this, the resistance to doing it can be surprisingly strong. It is easy to underestimate the effects of delusion on motivation. *Moha* inclines the mind towards the status quo and one of its powerful weapons is inertia. It doesn't want things to change, and consciousness or awareness are precursors to positive change.

Becoming more aware of *moha* itself is key to being able to work with our minds more effectively.

Along with the unclear, confusing, and undermining (to our practice) aspects of delusion there is another dimension whose outward appearance is quite different.

Watch Out for False Certainty

Recently a good friend of mine described (due to a mix-up in communication) his experience of being a third wheel on a supper date. His two dinner companions had met to discuss human-made climate change, an issue on which they stood on opposite sides of a significant and often heated debate. They each made their points strongly and didn't hold back from clear disagreement or stating where they thought there had been bias, insufficient research, or unclear thinking on the part of the other. And yet my friend came away from the meal deeply impressed with the friendly tone of the communication and the respectful attention each had given to the other's argument. No minds were changed though positions softened, and each took something away from the meeting to reflect upon.

Why was my friend so impressed? Well, because what he witnessed is so hard to do.

Think of those occasions where you disagree with someone: you're just not going to back down because you really believe in what you're saying; it matters to you a lot. Things start to get a little heated as you both reassert your points of view even more strongly. Even if you remain polite, with the outward appearance of reasonableness, you might feel your shoulder muscles getting tight and your voice and emotions mirroring your body. Before you know it, you are slicing and dicing their perspective with a very sharp metaphorical knife!

When we feel we're right about something, by extension we put others in the wrong. Once we've done that it's difficult to have an open dialogue where we appreciate a good conversation. We're much more likely to try to change their mind rather than really listen to what the other person says. One of the characteristics of this side of *moha* is inflexibility. We get stuck on a single point of view and then we're not open to other possibilities.

There is a relationship between certainty and wrong view which Sangharakshita brings out in his teachings on Right View. Right View, he says, when held with tightness and the feeling of being right, is actually wrong view. When we take up and hold on to a position of any kind, whether it be 'breakfast is essential' or 'there is no "self"', we remain caught in a polarization between something 'right' and something else that is 'wrong'.

When we hold tightly to anything, we are in a dualistic relationship to it, with the basic delusion being that there *is* a me who holds tightly to the things *I* want, or *I* think or feel. The mind of wisdom is free from position and view, which is why Right View at this higher, third level of wisdom is also referred to as No View. There is no mental positioning from which we come, no individualized point of view. No View has its own limitations as a description of the awakened mind, as it is perhaps difficult for us from our deluded consciousness to conceive of having clarity without it resting on a position or stating that position.

As human beings, we like to know where we stand. Uncertainty plays into doubts and particularly self-doubt, which we can find very uncomfortable to be with. The more certain we can be, even about trivial things, the more in control we feel, and the less insecure. You only have to look at the food and beverage industry to see the plethora of views it's possible to be 'right' and 'wrong' about: everyone should have breakfast, fasting is good for you, coffee is bad for you, being underweight is as unhealthy as being overweight! The views and opinions are endless, as is the desire to *know what to do*. At the bottom of all these small moments of looking for security and to fix unimportant things is the much more significant desire to pin down our own fluid and transient nature into something controllable, and clearly defined as 'me'.

I have noticed this tendency with the broken collar bone I talked about in an earlier chapter. I was given minimal instructions to cover the period from initial diagnosis to the return visit to the fracture clinic six weeks later. So, as my symptoms unfold in unexpected ways (never having broken a bone before, I have no experience of what to expect), I've been seeking out more information from Dr Google. I know this is not a good thing to do (a friend once wryly remarked that every medical enquiry on the Internet ends in death) – there is so much conflicting information that it is impossible to find out if I'm doing the right thing. Should I wear the sling for six weeks/a few days/all the time/not at night? Do I exercise through the pain or not, if the exercises hurt more than not exercising? Should I raise my arm above my head or not more than seventy degrees out from my body? The Internet is a minefield of contradictory possibilities.

At the bottom of it *I want to know what to do* so that *my* shoulder heals properly, so that I can go back to living my life as I did before with trouble-free shoulders. I want to be able to carry on swimming and cycling and cooking. Plus, I'd like to go back to typing with more than one finger and all the other things that constitute *me* and *my* life!

It becomes very interesting to notice our desire for certainty. We can watch out for absolute thinking and views such as 'she *always* criticizes me' and 'he *never* does the washing up', fuelled by unrecognized friends of craving, aversion, and ignorance. It can be interesting to notice where you label things right or wrong? Or good or bad? It's helpful to actively look to see the other side of an argument rather than let the mind settle into a single stance.

When we are aware of making an assumption or expressing absolute certainty about something, we can start to recognize that our strong opinions are based on a whole mishmash of things, such as our views and emotions, that in themselves are not trustworthy or reliable. Because they are conditioned by ignorance, they are often based on nothing better than highly selective and inaccurate perceptions.

When we fail to recognize this, we allow *moha* free range. If we can be aware that what seems so right is simply our own point of view and not the truth, it allows for more wisdom as well as humility. We are less likely to dig in to cement our own perspective and close off other ideas and perspectives. When we recognize our own point of view more objectively, we are also able to then work more collaboratively and cooperatively with others.

The Role of Assumptions

A useful thing to watch out for is how often you assume something. Assumptions are generally about what is happening in the present but they're implicit views we're not usually conscious of. They are often unconscious biases in the mind, quite hidden from the self we like to project. We might assume that someone doesn't like us because they won't meet our eye, or that someone is stupid because they speak with a different accent to us. Even positive assumptions – that someone is competent or clever – will be based on our own views about what a competent person should look or sound like. Assumptions close us down to an actuality and are part of the world we run in our heads.

Assumption's partner in crime is 'speculation', which tends to be more future oriented and is also delusive as it's based on things that can't be known in that moment. I try to make a practice of noticing whenever the mind speculates, even about something as innocuous as the weather. 'I wonder if we'll have sunshine tomorrow?' In the speech precepts that I took on at the time of my ordination into the Triratna Order, this would come under useless speech. It can seem harmless, but it perpetuates the delusive mind. Actually, we can only ever know what is happening right now.

Sometimes our assumptions and speculations are much more harmful, as when we speculate about other people's motives rather than asking them directly. This can cause significant misunderstandings between individuals, with many friendships and marriages floundering on the rocks of assumptions or presumptions. We get ourselves into a whole heap of trouble through assuming we know what someone else means or thinks or feels. Once we've assumed something, without awareness, it is a tiny mental step to start to proliferate, eventually building a whole world of fabrication on top of something that we don't know is true to start with. Even more dangerous are the misunderstandings between communities and countries which can have global consequences.

Daniel Kahneman talks of how 'people are brilliant at creating a narrative from minimal evidence' and goes on to describe the brain as 'a machine for jumping to conclusions'![4] If we can notice every time we find ourselves saying or thinking 'I wonder. . .' or 'I hope. . .', we go some way to catching ourselves mid-jump and have the opportunity to become more conscious of the faulty basis to our thinking. We then buy in less to the story that follows on from it.

All of this secondary reality in the form of assumptions and presumptions, of concepts and rigid certainties, can be creatively worked with by attending to our present moment experience. Our direct experience is always there, always accessible, pointing us towards what is *actually* happening, rather than our ideas about experience.

When we attend to sounds, sights, touch, and how the mind is feeling in any moment, we re-set a better balance between the world of concepts and a world of direct experience. The idea of 'rain' is secondary to the sound, and it's the same with the 'flower' that is simply seen in awareness. As we tune into processes of mind such as 'thinking', 'remembering', or 'knowing', we resist diving into the content of those thoughts and memories and being carried away far beyond what's occurring now.

Recognizing Wisdom at Work

If we're reminding ourselves to be aware and checking for Right View, we're doing all that's needed to set up the conditions for wisdom to arise at some point. Awareness and Right View will enable us to make use of the information we've taken in and use its natural intelligence to skilfully watch the mind. The more we let the observing mind do its own work, the less tempted we will be to try and interfere to *make* something happen. We begin to become familiar with how the mind feels when it is seeing more clearly, and the receptive, kind, and sane quality to it.

Each time we recognize the wisdom quality working in the mind, it becomes easier to notice it again. We sense the way wisdom thinks and feels in the mind and what its characteristics are. Every time the mind knows an object clearly, or we understand the *nature* of some aspect of the mind, and we recognize that *understanding* and *knowing* as the wisdom mind, we encourage its growth and deepening.

It takes a certain amount of faith in the practice to persevere when not much seems to be happening or when the mind is full of unpleasant objects such as physical pain or mental suffering. And there are plenty of times when this will be the case – our bias is set to orient towards the pleasant – but it is an inevitable part of being human. It may well be that wisdom is quite weak at times and we don't have much perspective on what's happening. Practice can feel as if we are head down, walking into a storm. Sometimes all we can do is just keep going and do our best to recognize what's needed in that moment to strengthen awareness and the skilful qualities of mind and heart.

Keeping going doesn't mean grimly and rigidly doing the same thing that isn't working for us. Taking a break or a walk can help the mind wake up or relax and open. We keep being aware but choose the conditions that support well-being in a broad sense. If we understand that one of the most important conditions is to persevere, and we just keep on gently persisting while being mindful of objects being known in awareness, at some point that will bear fruit.

When we have some momentum in awareness, and Right View is working in the mind more naturally, our perspective can start to change, and we see differences in how we relate to things and people in our lives. This can give us the confidence to bring this hands-off approach of receptivity and non-interference to other difficulties and habits.

Wisdom and Delusion

It is not enough to understand wisdom without also understanding the forces of delusion in the mind. We may have clear moments when the mind understands the ephemeral nature of all experience, but without also understanding *through direct observation* how the mind constructs and fabricates its world through our sense experiences, our insights will have limited impact. We have to integrate our insights into our lives before they can really be said to be wisdom. Ultimately, it is not even possible to understand the wisdom nature without understanding the very depths of our ignorance.

This is why there is such an emphasis in the practice of watching the mind to recognize the conditioned factors of the body-mind; we look inwards to understand the mechanisms deep in the mind that cause us to act, speak, and think in deluded ways. We see the depths of our self-interest and self-referential nature, and become intimate with the ways it causes us suffering. When we bring Right View into the observing awareness, *wisdom is already there*. It may be necessary to see the same destructive habit of resentment, impatience, or boredom a thousand times before some deep understanding dawns . . . but don't be discouraged by this. In the image I used at the beginning of this chapter of the piece of fabric with light shining on it, each moment of seeing clearly causes a tiny rent in the cloth. Each tear represents some learning and more awareness brought to a pattern of mind and heart.

It helps if we can let the mind be satisfied with simplicity. Patience and acceptance open the mind to an interest in *whatever* is there. Awareness is awareness whatever it is observing, and when it works with Right View the mind will be collecting information or pieces of our jigsaw puzzle that eventually reveals a fuller picture. We can't *make* the mind be wise, and we can't force the intuitive connections necessary for insight, but we can set up the best conditions possible. We can't know when or where, or under what conditions wisdom will arise. We just need to practise as best we can with steadiness, curiosity, and receptivity.

Mindful Pause: Recognizing Wisdom and Delusion in the Mind

Settle into a comfortable posture that supports relaxation and awareness in body and mind. If your eyes are open, let them soften rather than actively looking at whatever the gaze is falling on.

Notice when you are with your experience in the present moment and when you've been caught up with an object of the senses including the mind sense.

Keep reminding yourself to be aware in a calm and spacious way, welcoming another moment as another moment to be aware.

Without actively seeking, can you recognize any manifestations of delusion in the mind? This might be the hazy or vague mind that isn't able to know objects clearly or the 'don't know' mind of confusion. Beware of any knee-jerk reaction to try harder to see more clearly. The aim is simply to be aware of how delusion manifests and not to attempt to make it go away.

You might notice the false certainty of some thoughts or assumptions in the mind. How does it feel to recognize these subtle mind objects?

Is there anything else the mind can notice that has the flavour of *moha*, of delusion?

Let more of your attention be with the mind that is knowing and recognizing objects including delusion. Rest with the knowing quality of mind.

At times, you might notice a gentle clarity in the mind, as if the mind is knowing more but with less effort.

Can you identify moments that have a stronger sense of clearly knowing? Recognize different facets of the wisdom mind.

Notice how the wisdom mind feels. What are its qualities? See how wisdom relates to other objects, and the mind itself.

Learn from wisdom nature in the mind. Does it look at things differently to your usual mind-set?

Become familiar with the taste and flavour of freedom in the wise mind.

Mindful Life Moment: Taking the Red Pill

When the film *The Matrix* was brought out in 1999, many of my friends were very excited and talked about it as a 'Buddhist film'. I'm not sure I agree, but I do think it works well as an allegory for aspects of the spiritual life. Here is a take on just a few aspects of it.

The Matrix – you may remember – starts off in a dull, human, humdrum world. It's a world that the main character, Neo, has never quite believed in and he seeks to uncover the 'truth'. In Neo's search there are echoes of the Buddha's and many a Dharma practitioner's lament: 'Is this all there is?' There must be more.

Neo's search leads him to a meeting with the mysterious and charismatic Morpheus. His intuitive doubts are affirmed, and he is offered a chance to see a truer reality. He is warned by Morpheus that it won't be easy, and there will be no turning back. Two pills are set in front of him and he can choose just one. The red pill, Morpheus says, will show him an unimaginable reality. It will show him the truth. However, if he takes the blue pill he will forget he's ever met Morpheus and will carry on with his regular life.

He takes the red pill.

There is a similar choice to be made in our Dharma lives. We can see the red pill as standing for wisdom, for seeing more clearly how things 'really' are. And the blue pill represents ignorance, the habit of wilful of self-delusion.

The character of Cypher is a vivid depiction of this self-delusion. He wants out of the dangers, difficulties, and sheer dreariness of 'true reality' and so he strikes a bargain with his oppressors (of the blue pill false reality). He'll betray his red pill companions if he can return to complete forgetting. He mouths the old cliché 'ignorance is bliss, right?' to the sinister Mr Smith, and insists he wants his 'rebirth' to be as someone rich and powerful, perhaps an actor. He is happy to live in a false reality as long as it is one of ease and pleasure and where he has (the illusion of) control.

For us, this choice is not just one decision to live a different kind of life, with new goals and changed values. Often it is a slow process from initial toe dabbling in a spiritual life to deep immersion, with a million tiny moments altering our perspective and softening our hearts along the way. Some days, we take the red pill; other days, we unthinkingly pop a blue one. As we learn more about how to practise well, we more consistently choose wisdom and love over greed and delusion.

I find it fascinating that once Neo is within the new 'reality' he is still basically the same person. Being there has opened his mind but it hasn't changed his behaviour at all. There is a parallel here with our leading and trailing edges in practice; or, to put it another way, vision and transformation. We may have some wisdom, but it can take time and further practice for it to work through, influencing our actions, speech, and mind.

Like us, Neo must learn to live to his full potential. He can defy gravity, if he believes it is possible! Morpheus is his teacher and his main work is to help Neo see the conditioned limits he imposes on himself. We too have to learn how to recognize the conventional reality we're constantly constructing around us and see beyond it.

Morpheus urges Neo to 'free your mind' – something we can connect with in every moment when we remind ourselves to be aware with Right View.

Chapter eight

Uncontrived Mindfulness
Bringing It All Together

You are not a good meditator. Awareness is good![1]

In this final chapter, we'll explore what happens when mindfulness and Right View have been cultivated to the extent that they have become more natural to the mind. When, through previous practice, the mind has been brought to the point where awareness is more seamless, other explorations become possible. We experience some fruits from our gentle yet persistent efforts. We will still notice various objects of experience, but awareness and Right View have strengthened enough to take them in their stride. Even unpleasant objects can be known from the unbiased and impersonal perspective of wisdom.

When the conditions are there that support awareness and wisdom being present in our experience more of the time, we can say there is momentum in practice. Mindfulness becomes 'uncontrived' in the sense that it unfolds naturally with minimal effort; and awareness with wisdom are seemingly working on their own, independent of self-direction.

With receptive mindfulness the mind can still feel quite ordinary and not far away from our usual consciousness, but if you make this mind the object of awareness, you'll see that there are some differences. The continuity brings a settled quality to the mind; it naturally chooses to be present rather than disappearing into imagined futures and remembered past events. Often the mind will feel sharp and quick; you might find your own words for describing how it feels. In conversation with my partner he spoke about the mind feeling very clear, whereas my experience was of being able to notice much greater subtlety. When we talked further, it was clear we were describing the same sort of experience.

Awareness and wisdom have come together in this quite ordinary and yet extraordinary quality of mind through cultivating mindfulness and bearing in mind the four aspects of Right Mindfulness: mindfulness, clear knowing, helpful effort, and the mind that is free from desires and discontent. We've been using those qualities as guides that help the mind to recognize *how* we are aware. The invitation has been to check to see if we're aware, and to notice the quality of awareness. It is also important to check regularly to see how we're relating to experience and notice whether Right View is present in our experience. We've been encouraging the growth of awareness through lightly dropping in such questions as 'Am I aware?' 'Is mindfulness present?' Through these questions we are *reminding* ourselves to be aware.

As well as looking at what happens when practice is going well, we'll look too at some of the pitfalls that limit practice developing fully.

Ways We Focus on Unawareness

Before looking more at how mindfulness can be 'uncontrived', we'll focus on what can happen after we've been lost in unawareness and then find ourselves once more in the present moment. We'll look at some habits of mind that make it easy to get in our own way and miss the opportunity to take the practice deeper.

Something you may have noticed during meditation practice is when mindfulness seems to spontaneously re-arise. You might notice this during the times when you 'wake up' out of being lost in a story, or when you hear or read about awareness and it triggers the experience of being aware. There may well be other triggers that you don't identify, but you know that you've moved from not being aware to being aware.

It can be very interesting to see what happens then. What do you do? Is it as simple as noticing that mindfulness wasn't there and now it's back again?

Often something else happens in the mind that creates a ruffle of agitation. The knowing of awareness becomes entangled in a reaction to having caught ourselves not being aware. See if you recognize any of the following ways the mind responds:

- *We judge the moment.* We think 'I haven't been aware' or 'I lost mindfulness'. The thoughts by themselves are fine but sometimes they are more than a simple acknowledgement of what has been happening and there can be a harsh judging quality to the thoughts. There might be a tightening or tensing in the mind and body, a curbing effect, as if we're trying to stop ourselves thinking. At this point, we're not able to be receptive to what's happening, we're trying to control the mind. It can lead to berating ourselves and our practice as 'not good enough', which in turn can lead into strong habits of further judgements.

- *We think about the moment.* 'Why did I lose awareness?' We look back to what was happening when we were unaware, rather than recognizing that mindfulness is again right there and present. If we focus on unawareness, we are likely to become lost in the content of our thoughts. 'What was I thinking about?' Even if we don't get lost, we are still focusing on unawareness, and missing the advantages of mindfulness having re-arisen.

- *We become despondent* about having been lost and believe a thought like 'oh, I should finish meditating now, I'm just distracted'. Again, we're focusing on the past unawareness rather than the present awareness. And further, we're allowing the *content* of the thought to determine our practice rather than simply recognizing a thought happening in awareness. We have forgotten to stay with the actual experience in the moment.

- We *try to do* something with the moment. 'OK, I'm back. I'm aware!' We over-exert through trying to do something. The attention can have a 'snatch and grab' quality to it. We do too much, and we miss the natural awareness that is already there without the extra and unnecessary personal effort.

It is good practice to notice any of the above and we can learn a lot through recognizing how we get in the way of awareness. In each of the scenarios it is helpful to check the quality of awareness and notice if Right View is present. Each moment is an opportunity to learn how the mind is working and to notice habits that hinder clear recognition of what is happening. When awareness is up and running it can notice habits of mind more quickly and understand more about the cause-and-effect processes in the mind – how the mind is working. With Right View working alongside awareness, the faculty of clear seeing moves from being an intermittent flash of knowing to a steadier illumination of the mental and emotional habits that lead to either suffering or freedom.

Once we have noticed the ways in which we focus on unawareness, it becomes easier to just be with present moment mindfulness. Awareness can re-arise without being pulled back into thinking about what has previously happened and, rather, staying with the current moment. This allows a smoother transition between times of unawareness and awareness.

The Dharma teacher Andrea Fella talks about 'the comings and goings of mindfulness'[2] and I think this is a helpful perspective. The more we can allow the mind to go with its own rhythm, the more we learn to trust and understand that awareness and wisdom arise on the basis of certain causes and conditions. We stop worrying about trying to maintain awareness through effort but, as best we can, put conditions in place – such as interest and receptivity – to support awareness.

In my own practice during times of some momentum, it has been helpful to understand that in order to have more continuity of mindfulness, I need to be willing for awareness to *not* be there at times. When I'm more relaxed around losing awareness, and less concerned with trying to hold on and keep it, it's more likely to stay. And when awareness is lost, and there is ease around that, it's likely to re-arise more quickly.

Uncontrived Mindfulness

As Natural as Breathing

Noticing the pitfalls above will allow more continuity of awareness as there are fewer diversions focusing on *not being aware*. This tends to make mindfulness smoother. A vital skill here is learning to 'coast' and ride the waves of practice rather than falling back into familiar and seductive habits of doubt and judgement. Or, when we fall in, we know how to get back up into the arms of awareness as soon as we can. In this way, we are *aware* of what's happening, which brings crucial spaciousness and objectivity to compelling thoughts and believable feelings.

Awareness cannot thrive in an atmosphere of tension and attempts to control it. If we want to access a more stable awareness in order to watch more subtle aspects of the mind, relaxation and enjoyment are crucial.

We settle into a calmer and more easeful way of seeing, using very little energy to just notice what is happening. We can just be present and interested in the reappearance of awareness. It comes and it goes, and when we become aware of its re-arising, we observe the differences in the mind between awareness and unawareness.

We become familiar with the flavour of awareness naturally re-arising, and we start to see how often it happens that mindfulness arises and is present. We are able to see the effortless quality to being aware. It's just happening by itself; no one is doing it.

Mindfulness becomes something noticed, rather than something we do. It is as natural as breathing. We breathe in the scent of awareness. We taste its flavour. We appreciate the mind that is able to be aware.

Being Sensitive to What's Needed – Using Appropriate Effort

There is an archetypal figure running through most of the Buddhist traditions named Vajrapāṇi (the protector of the diamond thunderbolt). His wrathful form is a deep midnight blue colour with attendant garlands of skulls, and he wears a tiger skin around his waist. Unusually for Buddha and Bodhisattva figures, he starts off life as a *'yakṣa'* – a slightly malign nature spirit – but progresses over time to the stature of a fully Enlightened Buddha.

Vajrapāṇi symbolizes energy directed to whatever is wholesome and beneficial. He has tremendous strength and power which is informed by wisdom. His figure represents great energy, but I've always been more interested in the skilfulness required to use the energy or effort in ways *appropriate* to what's needed. With great power, an even greater sensitivity is required to use strong energy in ways that benefit rather than cause harm. Without sensitivity, power can *overpower* or overwhelm, and this creates pushback in the form of resistance.

As we've seen in earlier chapters, nowhere is this more obvious than with the mind. If we use too much energy or try too hard at the wrong time, the mind immediately becomes tight and transmits tension to the body. Our thinking too can contribute to tension. Thoughts can come with a lot of power of conviction and without enough awareness, we easily believe them. They may not be true, and not necessarily helpful to practice, so it is vital to notice them with awareness present.

Knowing how much energy to use, and how to use it well, means we don't become overcommitted in any one direction but can remain responsive to what is needed. I used to practise the martial art aikido, and while aikido can be very strong and vigorous, the same fluidity and responsiveness is a core principle. We are not committed to defending from the front or the back of the body, or either side. The physical stance is always balanced and light so that we can move in whatever direction an attack comes from. One of the strengths of receptive mindfulness is its flexibility – *anything*, any object, can be known in awareness, just like the butterfly, landing so lightly, on the leaf or on the moment. Similarly, it just takes the lightest quality of attention, remembering to notice until it becomes so natural for the mind to do so that it remembers on its own.

One of the things you might notice is that although you feel happy and settled in practice, you are aware of more objects than before. It would be easy think that you are getting distracted rather than calmer and steadier. This conclusion can lead you to apply strategies to remedy the situation, or even to put more effort in to counter this 'busy' mind. This would be a misunderstanding of what is happening in your practice.

One of the signs that awareness is growing is that you find it easier to notice more objects in rapid succession. If you can observe while still feeling settled back and relaxed, it means that your awareness is gaining momentum and naturally taking in more through the senses. The awareness itself is steady and the objects of mind can just carry on doing what they do, seeing and hearing, tasting etc. The objects might not change that much but it is as if we've become fluent in noticing them and so we land on them very lightly, allowing more 'weight' to rest with the knowing mind. It becomes natural for awareness to be interested in the quality of mind.

At times like this there can be a sense of flow, and the awareness can feel panoramic, as if the mind is knowing objects from all the senses surrounding it. Even though objects are known quickly and almost simultaneously, it can seem as if awareness has slowed right down, taking everything in with grace and ease.

Because the *observing* mind is steady it can notice much more of what is happening in the momentary arisings through the senses, including the mind sense. When there is enough continuity of moments of mindfulness, you can notice much more. Of course, it is not really 'you' but awareness noticing objects. Whereas when awareness was sporadic, it missed a lot of sights, sounds, and other sense experiences, once it's more continuous you see that there are always things happening and you see the flow of objects through different senses. It is really a very good sign when you have the sense that 'you' are not doing anything, but awareness is noticing many objects of experience. Of course, the point is not to notice as many objects as you can, but that this type of panoramic or global mindfulness is an indication that awareness has become well established.

At this point, we may find we need to use even less effort than we have been doing! Too much energy or effort can stop the mindfulness and wisdom progressing by causing us to get in our own way. When there is momentum in the practice, you need to be very aware of the amount and quality of effort you use. It is a good idea to regularly check how little effort you can use and still be aware.

You may find there is no longer any need to remind yourself to be aware but just to check every now and again that mindfulness is 'working' in the mind. Often, we can see that we're already aware before the thought to remind ourselves arises. In fact, the thought is prompted by the awareness that is already present.

Another factor that can tempt us to put in too much effort at this stage is, ironically, when we recognize that practice is going well. There can be a rush of enthusiasm that can replace awareness. So, watch the mind carefully when you find you really want to apply yourself to the practice. It might be that eagerness has caused awareness and right effort to be usurped by craving and the wanting mind. Remember, awareness has patience and lets the conditions build naturally in the mind, whereas craving is keen to try and *make* things happen.

When we notice ease and balance in the mind that is observing and recognizing, we need *less* effort rather than more. The mind is a sensitive instrument, and awareness a subtle faculty. By over-exerting we easily knock awareness out of the picture as we become identified with a more personal effort. Instead we need to continue to notice the conditions that support awareness to arise and be sensitive to what is needed as mindfulness develops more momentum.

On the Edge of the Mystery of Awareness

Earlier in the book I mentioned David Attenborough in relation to his response of wonder and receptivity to the natural world. The same qualities can subtly inform our practice as we become familiar with awareness becoming more continuously available. We can find that our experience is pleasantly unfamiliar, even a little bit mysterious. Perhaps we're coming to the limits of our usual state of consciousness. If we can stay, and open to the limits of what we know – which is really not very much – we're on the edge of the realm of mystery.

Sangharakshita describes this very beautifully in his essay on 'Pauses and Empty Spaces':

When the composer Mozart was asked what was the most important part of his music, he did not reply that melody, or harmony, or counterpoint, or even orchestration was the most important, but simply 'the pauses'.

So, in the paintings of the Far Eastern – Chinese and Japanese - masters of the art of landscape, it is the empty spaces which are the most important parts of the picture. The vast empty spaces of sky, or snow, or water are not only themselves charged with mysterious significance as a cloud with lightning, but they somehow infuse that significance into the single blossomless branch or tiny floating boat, or solitary human figure at the edge . . . of the huge blank expanse of paper. . .

And just as the pauses are the most important part of music and the empty spaces the most important part of a picture, so are silence and emptiness the most important part of life. A life which consists of a frantic stream of external activities, without one moment of inward recollection, is like music which is an uninterrupted succession of sounds, or a picture which is crammed with figures. . .

As music is born of silence, and derives its significance therefrom; and as a painting is born of empty space, and derives its significance therefrom; so are our lives born of silence, of stillness, of quietude of spirit, and derive their significance, their distinctive flavour and individual quality, therefrom. The deeper and more frequent those moments of interior silence and stillness wherein, transcending all sights and sounds, tastes and touches, we experience Reality as it is, the more rich in significance, the more truly meaningful, will our lives be. . . .

It is the pauses which make beautiful the music of our lives. It is the empty spaces which give richness and significance to them. And it is the stillness which makes them truly useful.[3]

We may touch this sense of openness or mystery occasionally or regularly in our lives. If you are an artist of any kind, or a musician or a writer, you might be familiar with having no idea of what comes next, or where you're going with your story, painting, or composition. You might know, through having come to this place many times before, that you need to be patient, to not push, and to see what happens next.

In 1934, the psychologist Marion Milner wrote a book called *A Life of One's Own* where, through wondering why she isn't happier, she starts to watch her mind and keep a diary of what she learns. She describes in the most beautiful way how she stumbles onto what we call mindfulness. She learns to watch her mind and discovers a gap between her habitual thoughts and something new, an 'inner gesture', which leads her to feel quite differently about her life. She describes how she moves from her usual thinking mode into a more receptive mood and what happens as she starts to write:

> How curious . . . I must have no enthusiasm, no pride in whether I can do it. There seems always to be a feeling of futility that I have nothing to say and usually I try to get away from this by force, by looking for something to say . . . But if I can accept this futility and give up my purpose to write and yet don't run away into some other activity, just sit still . . . then the crystallisation begins.[4]

When we touch on this experience in meditation, it can feel somewhat risky to simply be aware in this extended pause. Often thoughts and feelings will discourage us from staying with an experience which seems to be going nowhere. It can bring up the thought that nothing will happen or the fear that we're wasting our time, but if we can stay in this extended pause and recognize doubts and thoughts for what they are, we can find ourselves in the territory of mindfulness that is uncontrived and unfabricated.

When we hold ourselves in suspension, without forcing, as Marion Milner says, often something comes that is new and fresh to us. We couldn't have articulated it before that moment of waiting, of holding ourselves open. New ways of seeing come to us like a gift. They shift our perspectives and open us to a clearer recognition of the uncontrived nature of awareness where we can recognize the impersonal and fabricated nature of all we experience. We learn to stay with the mystery of awareness and let go of the ceaseless impulse to pin things down.

Sometimes, in this space, a question arises in the mind which we didn't consciously think but which comes about through wisdom's influence. The question arises from the unfamiliar perspective of awareness and wisdom and impacts on how we look at things. One such question that has been fruitful for me is 'How do I know I'm aware?' I'm not trying to find an answer but rather to provoke joyful interest and further inquiry into the direct experience of the body-mind. Wisdom doesn't travel in a straight line seeking an answer but opens the mind like a flower unfurling its petals, perhaps revealing something unseen until that moment of attending.

In most of our lives, by necessity, we have an agenda. We have things to do, and things we ought to be doing. We have 'to do' lists filling our days, and many different stimulating and distracting ways to fill our minds. They may be worthy things or mindless things; interestingly, the effect on us is often barely distinguishable – our minds are stuffed full of thoughts and images, anxieties and fantasies. We endlessly plan and busily make arrangements, giving ourselves little opportunity to simply be present to ourselves and our world in that moment. It is incredibly restful and nourishing for the mind to pause its ceaseless mental action and touch into the mysterious nature of all that we don't know. It impacts positively on both our desire to live a happy, healthy, human life, and as a basis for the mind to open deeply into wisdom.

Journeying into the Dark

Beyond preparing the mind and heart by encouraging a loving, open awareness, we don't really know where we're going in our practice. If we are always directing the mind to where we want it to go, we remain with what is already known to us and we can't step out of our own paradigm. Our training in mindfulness and Right View encourages us to stand on the edge of what we can know directly and then to see what happens. By doing so, we open into the mystery beyond. Through mindfulness we are looking to access that which is beyond what we've known through our conceptual faculties.

If we accept that Enlightenment is beyond our understanding, how do we think we'll get there? We can't know what Enlightenment or Awakening is, though we're told it will lead to an understanding and resolving of all that causes us to feel dis-ease and dissatisfaction. We need to find ways, set up conditions, and invite in that which allows us access to that which is beyond what we already know. We do this through using the conditioned world to understand what is beyond it. We – or rather, wisdom – find a new way of looking at the same old world, and the understanding that arises sets us free.

It can be a necessary humbling experience to realize we don't know what we're doing or where we're going. That, however we imagine Awakening to be, however we conceive of it, is not it. Until insight is present, all we have is simply a conception, an idea about the goal of the spiritual life. We are in the dark, spiritually speaking, and whatever we try to hold on to turns to dust in our hands. Ironically, when we understand this, we are closer to an insightful appreciation of the value of our present moment experience.

A key is our ability to pay attention to the direct experience of our senses, which includes the mind sense with its capacity to know and to be aware. Right View and awareness allow our horizons to broaden so that we get a glimpse of a new way of being that has previously been unfamiliar and unknown to us. It is as if we're learning to discern another rhythm to our lives. Beneath the hustle and bustle of work, family and play, and even practice is a rhythm that is more restful, like a steady heartbeat. It is akin to the stillness and vibrancy we might experience through being in nature or hearing beautiful music.

The difference in our practice is that we don't need external factors such as a beautiful environment to bring this other rhythm about; we can use our own mind and mental faculties. Awareness and Right View come together to influence how we experience the nature of the mind, and so we come to know awareness and its objects as simply another moment of impersonal conditioned arising.

Aware of Awareness

With continuity of awareness, it becomes possible to explore more fully *being aware that you're aware*. Not only are we aware of the objects of experience, but we *know* that we're aware of them. This knowing has a palpable, almost physical sense to it; the awareness is able to know that it is aware as well, as recognizing the objects of that same awareness. The experience of knowing the awareness can become very clear to the mind, so that we wonder how we didn't notice it before.

This is not an intellectual knowing but an ability to feel into each moment more fully and recognize *that which is knowing*. We can identify that there is both something that is *known* to the mind (the object) and something that is *knowing* (awareness or mind). And now there is a third element which is able to know both of knowing and known aspects of experience.

Exploring this territory within your experience can be very fruitful. With every object recognized you can start to more easily recognize the knowing quality of awareness. It can be fun to play with noticing the knowing – *that which knows* – quality in the mind, and the object – *that which is known*. You begin to see what you can notice about these functions of mind: how they differ, and what they're like from this more impersonal perspective that awareness and Right View bring.

In these times of recognizing awareness, it's important to remain receptive to what's happening and not look too hard. Remember, it is as if you're looking very softly out of the corner of the mind's eye. You let the observing remain relaxed and open, not looking *for* something, but noticing whatever is arising through the mind sense door.

When we look hard or try to see or understand, we are usually functioning on personal effort, effort that is driven by a sense of self wanting to know, to do, or to try. We haven't recognized that the mental factors of awareness and Right View have sufficient ongoing presence in the mind to render personal effort unnecessary. And too much effort can mean we miss various thoughts and feelings that coalesce into a sense of 'I'm' the one making the effort or wanting to practise well, and so on. But when the quality of awareness is working well it becomes clear that 'I' or 'me' is an extra mental construct that can be identified in awareness as such. Once we've clearly seen what's happening, we just need to let mindfulness and Right View continue under their own momentum.

Until awareness understands its own nature through continued investigation of mindfulness and wisdom working together, there will always be some delusion in the mind that continues to influence our experience. These delusive views and ideas are usually implicit and not consciously held, though they might also come from partial understandings of what we've read or experienced in our own practice. We may find it valuable to reflect and study so that we are clear on the intellectual framework of the Buddha's teachings, but it is even more important to practise with awareness and Right View, allowing them to understand as much as they can without any personal agenda on our part.

Even when we feel clear that objects such as body sensations or thoughts are 'not self', we often remain identified with awareness or the sense of knowing as 'me'. Implicit in the mind is the wrong view or idea that it is *me* who is aware, who is knowing. When we are able to recognize mindfulness more consistently and know that we're aware, this sense of self becomes more apparent and easier to observe. Whenever we spot 'selfing' in relation to awareness we can observe it closely. We can notice what is happening in those moments of identifying with awareness and tune into exactly what it is that is being taken as 'me', as self. You can see how insubstantial and fleeting it is: a feeling in the mind, a few sensations in the body, or a continual referencing back to something that can't be found.

When these wrong ideas about, for example, the nature of consciousness, awareness, or experience are seen more clearly, these understandings liberate and brighten the mind, even if the clouds of misunderstanding come back in afterwards.

Whenever you find it accessible, stay with the awareness, rather than objects that awareness is knowing. Catch the quality of awareness gently out of the corner of the mind's eye and follow it like a golden thread.

Mindful Pause: Aware of Awareness

Find your way into a mind-body state that you feel some ease and naturalness with. Take all the time you need, enjoying the present moments.

Let the mind be very soft and open. See if you can be aware of that which is knowing whatever is happening, including knowing any resistance, tension, or unnecessary effort.

Settle back to be with the knowing quality of the awareness. Notice how it feels. What are its particular flavours or characteristics?

As you notice the mind moving to different objects and taking them in, look to stay with the awareness as it moves. Be with the movement. Notice the awareness arising with each new object.

The awareness doesn't precede the object; it's not lying in wait for something else to arise, another sound or sight, or mental object. Awareness knows, and the object is known – it happens at the same time.

Let the energy of the mind be light and playful as you explore awareness and object, knowing and known.

The more you can rest with the awareness and keep knowing it, the clearer the understanding of the mind/object relationship will be.

Uncontrived Mindfulness

When mindfulness starts to work on its own and we let go of controlling awareness in ever more subtle ways, the body and mind can start to relax deeply. There is often a significant decrease in mental and physical tension as the urge to direct and try greatly lessens. It can be a time when students recognize how much personal energy they're still using despite having reduced a lot of unnecessary effort. This is a delicate point in practice where we switch from relying on personal effort to sustain awareness, to trusting awareness and Right View to do their jobs without interference.

As mindfulness, working with Right View, become increasingly strong factors in the mind, they need very little prompting or reminding to keep going. Interest in the present moment is naturally there along with ease and calm in the observing mind. When we no longer need to put much personal energy into sustaining awareness and we know it is there much of the time, we can say there is momentum in the practice. It is no longer dependent on personal effort but sustains and deepens itself. That is not to say it will stay like this indefinitely, so we need to check the mind every now and again to see when the conditions change and, once again, we need to inject conscious interest or attention.

The more that we can step out of our own way and allow awareness and wisdom to do what they do best, we tap into a stream of mindfulness that is uncontrived and unfabricated. We are not contriving or perpetuating certain habit streams that demand to tell the same or a variant of the story of 'me'. Instead we allow them to be known in awareness without suppression or indulgence. Through clear, dispassionate observation we can see habits that tend the mind towards suffering calm down and the mind can be transformed through the quality of wise attention.

We can contrast uncontrived mindfulness with our general mode of being where we are continually fabricating or 'contriving' our experience into a solid and whole sense of self. What is fabricated is a small world around a self-referential centre. Uncontrived mindfulness, on the other hand, naturally re-arises moment after moment, allowing experience to simply unfold. There is nothing to hold onto. Awareness has become uncontrived and unprompted, imbued with wisdom factors of mind. The more consistently we can keep up this type of awareness working with wisdom, increasingly the mind will naturally know the *nature* of whatever is happening. If we can keep recognizing the *nature* of experience, over time there comes a point when it becomes impossible to misunderstand in our usual ways. The work of the Dharma will be done.

Conclusion

It takes a few days or weeks to read a book, but awareness and Right View are practices for life.

They involve a profound reorientation of how we live, from prioritizing a life of sense experiences which we take up and put down with glee or disgust, to knowing and becoming aware of those same sense experiences and our reactions to them. This takes a keen interest and ongoing diligence. It requires that we keep our sense of purpose and spiritual direction in mind, as if we were being guided by our own inner north star. Practising well also means being willing to begin again and again every time mindfulness is lost, even when we feel discouraged or unmotivated. Those mind states too can be noticed in awareness.

If there is one thing I would like to 'stick' with you more than any other, it is just how crucial it is to recognize *how* we are aware. This is the helpful perspective of Right View that enables us to recognize attitudes of mind that colour our perceptions and influence us, sometimes for better but frequently for worse. When we are able to do this, as Sayadaw U Tejaniya says, 'wisdom is working in the mind', a wisdom going back to the time of the Buddha.

I started the book by evoking the serenity of the Buddha talking with King Bimbisāra, pointing to the happiness of a life in awareness, and guided by wisdom and understanding. And I'll end with the 'lion's roar' of the Buddha expressing supreme confidence in the value of mindfulness and Right View. In the words of the *Satipaṭṭhāna Sutta*, the rewards for our efforts are the fruits of clear seeing and freedom from suffering, leading to the greatest peace:

Dharma Farer, this is the direct path for the purification of beings, for the surmounting of sorrow and lamentation, for the disappearance of dukkha and discontent, for acquiring the true method, for the realization of Nirvana, namely, the four Satipaṭṭhānas.[5]

Mindful Life Moment: Let What You Love Lead You to Wisdom

As I come to the end of writing this book, I've been reflecting on the process of writing about awareness and wisdom and why it has felt important to do so. When reflecting on my practice, sometimes I'll ask myself why I continue to practise in this way. What have I gained, how has my practice developed?

What comes to mind is a phrase that doesn't immediately answer the questions above but is more of a spontaneous utterance: *awareness is transformative*. Such simple words, they are almost a cliché. So, what do I mean by them? How does awareness transform, and what does it transform? It transforms through the power of 'knowing' and the scope of that which is known.

I believe that awareness can 'know' anything. Not everything, of course. Awareness is not omniscient. There may well be things happening in us or outside of us that we don't know. We miss hearing part of a conversation because we have some hearing loss, or we bang a door shut accidentally through not having realized it was windy outside. It's easy to confuse the capacity of awareness to know 'everything' with knowing 'anything'. Awareness means knowing anything that is already happening and registering somewhere in my experience.

I can be aware that 'hearing' is happening even as I register that I'm straining to make out a sound. That sense of strain can also be known in awareness, and the quality of the mind that is aware of straining is recognized without strain, and with the pleasure of present moment awareness. Awareness can know the whole process. The more awareness there is, the more clearly these things can be known.

To be aware of anything means that nothing is excluded from awareness. There are no exceptions or things we can't be aware of. Typically, the mind will prioritize thinking about something rather than being aware of it, often in its desire to either prolong or get rid of whatever it is worrying about, like a dog with a bone.

Experiencing with awareness, rather than thinking about a compelling inner story, or an overwhelming emotion such as fear or rage, means that in a small corner of my mind I know what's happening. If I can recognize and inhabit that space, scrunched down waiting and watching patiently while the rest of the picture plays out, awareness will grow and expand out of its corner to influence whatever else is happening. Once awareness has grown, even a little, there is some ease and spaciousness in the mind. Awareness helps the mind begin to recognize where it is 'caught' and identified with what is happening.

Recognizing identification is what awareness and wisdom do best. While the thinking mind will unhappily tie itself in knots trying to fix what is happening, in order to put it down, awareness and wisdom are willing to just 'know'. As well as knowing what's going on, we can also know how we are relating to the experience. If that is with identification, the wisdom element recognizes that this is what's happening and knows it is not necessary to struggle. Naming something helps to objectify it: this is fear, this is rage, this is what jealousy or longing feels like. But what's crucial is to notice the identification going alongside the feelings.

Awareness transforms by illuminating any aspect of experience it encounters; whatever I'm experiencing can be known in a way that (eventually) allows it to be stripped of clinging, and, therefore, of suffering. Nothing is outside the scope of wise attention.

When I look to why I still practise in this deceptively simple and yet profound way, what comes up are the memories of many moments of relief when the mind puts down what is causing it to suffer.

Notes and References

Introduction

1 Paraphrased from Anthony de Mello, *Awareness*, HarperCollins, London 1990.

2 Sangharakshita, *The Essential Sangharakshita*, Wisdom Publications, Boston 2009.

3 *Satipaṭṭhāna Sutta*, Anālayo translation from *Satipaṭṭhāna: The Direct Path to Realization*, Windhorse Publications, Birmingham 2003.

4 Ibid.

Chapter 1

1 Sangharakshita, *Peace is a Fire: A Collection of Writings and Sayings*, Windhorse Publications, Cambridge 1995.

2 David Wagoner, 'Lost', from *Travelling Light: Collected and New Poems*, University of Illinois Press, Champaign 1999.

3 *Satipaṭṭhāna Sutta*, Anālayo translation from *Satipaṭṭhāna: The Direct Path to Realization*, Windhorse Publications, Birmingham 2003.

4 Emily Hasler, 'Cartography for Beginners', *The Map Lover* (unpublished), available at https://allyourprettywords.tumblr.com/post/52228344228/cartography-for-beginners-emily-hasler, accessed on 4 August 2020.

5 Sangharakshita, public talk on the Diamond Sutra, 1969, talk 74, Free Buddhist Audio, available at https://www.freebuddhistaudio.com/audio/details?num=74, accessed on 4 August 2020.

Chapter 2

1 Sayadaw U Tejaniya, *Awareness Alone Is Not Enough*, self-published, May 2010.

2 Rumi, 'Bismillah', *The Essential Rumi*, translated by Coleman Barks, HarperOne, London 2004.

3 From Patrick Baigent, *The Path of Relaxation*, lulu.com, July 2015.

4 *Satipaṭṭhāna Sutta*, Anālayo translation from *Satipaṭṭhāna: The Direct Path to Realisation*, Windhorse Publications, Birmngham 2003.

5 Khenpo Tsultrim Gyamtso Rinpoche, 'Self-appearing Illusion', arranged by Jim Scott, 2012.

Chapter 3

1 Ajahn Chah, 'Sense Contact: The Fount of Wisdom', Dhamma talk, available at https://www.ajahnchah.org/book/Sense_Contact_Fount.php, accessed on 5 August 2020.
2 James Joyce, 'A Painful Case', in *Dubliners*, Grant Richards, London 1914.
3 Shenpen Hookham, *There's More to Dying than Death*, Windhorse Publications, Birmingham 2006.

Chapter 4

1 Sangharakshita, *Living with Awareness*, Windhorse Publications, Birmingham 2003.
2 Sayadaw U Tejaniya, group interviews, Myanmar.
3 Sangharakshita, *Living with Awareness*, Windhorse Publications, Birmingham 2003.
4 Anālayo, *Satipaṭṭhāna: The Direct Path to Realisation*, Windhorse Publications, Birmingham 2003.

Chapter 5

1 Saṃyutta Nikāya 35:93.
2 Jacob Needleman, *Money and the Meaning of Life*, Bantam Doubleday Dell, New York 1991.
3 Paul Brand and Philip Yancey, *Pain: The Gift Nobody Wants*, HarperCollins, London 1982.

Chapter 6

1 Sayadaw U Tejaniya, Jhana Grove retreat transcription, 2011.
2 Anthony de Mello, *One Minute Wisdom*, Bantam Doubleday Dell, New York 1985.
3 The actual quote is: 'I've lived through some terrible things in my life, and some of them actually happened.'
4 Heard quoted in a Dharma talk by Joseph Goldstein.
5 Sayadaw U Tejaniya, Jhana Grove retreat transcription, 2011.
6 Tom Lubbock, *Until Further Notice I am Alive*, Granta Books, London 2012.

Chapter 7

1 Sangharakshita, *Living Wisely*, Windhorse Publications, Cambridge 2014.
2 Sayadaw U Tejaniya, *Collecting Gold Dust*, self-published, 2019.
3 Subhuti, 'The Just Sitting Practice – An Introduction', Free Buddhist Audio, 2009, available at https://www.freebuddhistaudio.com/audio/details?num=OM814, accessed on 5 August 2020.
4 Daniel Kahneman, *Thinking, Fast and Slow*, Penguin, New York 2012.

Chapter 8

1 Sayadaw U Tejaniya, from the author's personal notes, retreat with Sayadaw U Tejaniya, Czech Republic, 2011.

2 Andrea Fella, 'The Comings and Goings of Mindfulness', various audio talks available from DharmaSeed.org, available at https://dharmaseed.org/talks/audio_player/20/39007.html, accessed on 5 August 2020.
3 Sangharakshita, extract from the essay 'Pauses and Empty Spaces', *Crossing the Stream*, 1987, Windhorse Publications, Birmingham 1996.
4 Marion Milner, *A Life of One's Own*, Chatto & Windus, London 1934.
5 *Satipaṭṭhāna Sutta*, Anālayo translation from *Satipaṭṭhāna: The Direct Path to Realization*, Windhorse Publications, Birmingham 2003.

Index

Introductory Note

References such as '178–79' indicate (not necessarily continuous) discussion of a topic across a range of pages. Wherever possible in the case of topics with many references, these have either been divided into sub-topics or only the most significant discussions of the topic are listed. Because the entire work is about 'mindfulness', the use of this term (and certain others which occur constantly throughout) as an entry point has been minimised. Information will be found under the corresponding detailed topics.

awareness (*cont.*)
  natural state of 11–31
  and object 54, 96
  objects of 61, 104, 195
  open 130, 205
  reasons for being aware 11–12
  receptive 113, 138
  revolutionary nature 11
  and Right View 100, 102, 106, 149,
    157, 162, 206–8, 211
  simple 27, 40
  what we are aware of 61–83
  and wisdom 6, 122–3, 162, 165,
    173–4, 196, 198, 213–14

babies 52–3, 73
balance 20, 50, 59, 101, 202
  better 187
bare knowledge 24–5, 50
beaches 59, 118, 128, 160
beauty 4, 11–13, 31, 59, 87, 104
beliefs 86, 90, 126, 139, 150, 157,
  160–1
bias 75–6, 96, 100, 155, 183, 186, 188
Bimbisāra, King 1–3, 9, 11, 52, 211
bird song 13, 53, 73
body 23, 60–6, 76–7, 92–4, 100–105,
  116–19, 121–4, 136–9
  and mind 3, 6, 27, 35, 79, 130, 141,
    210
  scans 110, 112
  sensations 26, 36, 95, 98, 117, 119,
    149, 153
bones 23, 110–12, 117, 185, 213
  collar 87, 117, 184
boredom 12, 16, 101, 133, 189
brain 29, 77, 155, 167–8, 186
Brand, Paul 135
breath 19, 21, 23–6, 36, 40, 79–80, 94, 98
  sensations 20–1, 24
breathing 13, 21, 27, 43, 62, 64, 92, 98
  awareness as natural as 199–202
Buddhist traditions 15, 18, 92, 143,
  170, 199, 225

cake 6, 42, 46, 127
  cream 120
capacity 20, 63, 76–7, 95, 97, 206, 213
cause-and-effect relationships 119,
  198

certainty, false 183–5, 190
change, inevitability 116–18
characteristics 113, 158, 177, 184, 187,
  209
chest 21, 40, 147
children 4, 76, 90, 118, 135, 137, 160
citta 76–7 *see also* mind
clearly comprehending 40–6, 55
clearly knowing 40–6, 55, 59, 85, 190
clichés 192, 213
clinging xiv, 11, 124, 162, 175, 214
clouds 158, 175, 177, 203, 208
coldness 66, 141
collar bone 87, 117, 184
colouring 101, 131, 159, 170
colours 3, 28, 77, 90, 101, 158, 160,
  176–7
compassion 6, 41–2, 120, 125, 169,
  182
comprehending, clearly 40–6, 55
compulsion 54, 100, 180
concentration 8, 25, 45, 54, 158, 169
conditionality 91–2
  and Right View 102–3
conditions 69–70, 73, 90–1, 102–3,
  114–15, 125, 129, 198
  external 25, 90, 103
  helpful 67, 182
confidence xiv, 50, 54, 120, 137, 157,
  170, 174
confusion 61, 68, 148, 178, 190
connections 43, 51, 70, 145, 171, 179
consciousness 13, 24, 29, 70, 95, 97,
  202, 208
  deluded 184
  reflexive 13, 95
  usual 97, 195
contentment 30, 35, 52–3, 55–6, 58,
  61, 85
  and ease 53, 56, 85
continuity 42, 49, 51, 103, 115, 195
  of attention 42, 51
  of awareness 50–1, 182, 199, 207
  of mindfulness 7, 175, 198, 201
  of moments 51, 201
  of purpose 41, 45
continuous awareness 42–3, 126
continuous mindfulness 24, 50
contraction 21, 62, 79, 96, 102, 161,
  163

experience (*cont.*)
  nature of 94, 116, 176
  objects of 24, 28–9, 78, 82, 88, 95–6,
    195, 201
  physical 23, 47, 64–5
  recognizing identification with
    106–7
external conditions 25, 90, 103

faculties 3, 20, 69, 198, 202, 206
  mental 143, 206
  thinking 20, 143
faith xiv, 77, 100, 129, 140, 170, 188
false certainty 183–5, 190
familiar sounds 79, 111
family 41, 78, 123, 128, 206
fantasizing 30, 66, 73, 123
fantasy 90, 123–4, 127, 205
feeling tone 8, 25, 62–3, 68–70, 73–5,
    78, 81
  conditioning 69–71
  use of awareness to investigate 72
feelings 68–9, 71–2, 74–5, 87–9, 102–
    4, 106–8, 134–7, 161–3
  pleasant 74, 76
  unpleasant 70, 75–6, 95
Fella, Andrea 198
fingers 18, 20, 47, 88, 135, 167, 180,
    185
fingertips 47, 70
fluidity 63, 94, 184, 200
focus 8, 17, 24, 26, 88, 101, 103, 106–7
  single 24, 26, 104
  on unawareness 196–8
food 1, 67, 82, 103, 117, 130–1, 158,
    184
force 30, 46, 51, 83, 103, 155, 188–9,
    204
form 63–5
formal meditation 7, 44, 156
freedom xiii–xiv, 11, 15, 118–19, 140,
    170, 175, 191
  from desires and discontent 52–5
friends 33, 39, 74–5, 79–80, 86, 127,
    183, 185
frustration 4, 54, 86, 133–4, 137–8
fun 33, 126, 177, 207
  mindfulness of having 80–1
functions 30, 59, 77, 93, 123, 143–4,
    177, 207

mental 78, 144
natural 72, 95, 156

gestures, inner 13–14, 178, 204
gifts xiii, 82, 135–6, 204, 225
goals 3, 15, 37, 41–2, 54, 125, 169, 171
Google 86, 185
grasping 3, 12, 83, 102, 176
greed 100, 107, 121–4, 126, 130, 139–
    40, 158, 166
growth 34, 91, 93, 115, 137, 159, 187,
    196
  spiritual 119
grumpiness 133–4
guides 6, 16–17, 30, 196

habits 38–9, 92–3, 100, 113, 115,
    136–7, 196, 198
  emotional 78, 198
  strong 122, 137, 197
hands, touching 47–8, 57
happiness 1–4, 9, 11, 53, 87, 93, 132,
    134
harmony 28, 203
headaches 30, 135
health xiv, 65, 86, 116, 136
heat 23, 47, 51, 82, 94, 137, 147
hindrances 43, 85, 121–2, 198
holidays 2, 134, 139
home 12, 82, 110, 128
humour 6, 167

identification 100, 102, 105–6, 108,
    160–4, 214
ignorance 86, 119, 170, 175–8, 185,
    188, 192
illnesses xiv, 154, 167
illusion 82, 115, 192
images 65, 68, 126–8, 143, 145, 147–8,
    169, 171
  mental 23, 62, 76, 128
impatience 131–2, 189
inattention 52, 75, 117
independence of mind 53
independent mind 138–40
India 77, 135, 226
  northern 9
inevitability of change 116–18
information 56, 62, 165, 172, 175, 185,
    187, 189

inner experience 41, 66, 167
inner gestures 13–14, 178, 204
inner world 12–13, 75, 144, 146
insights 4, 6, 85–6, 97, 124–5, 169, 174–5, 188–9
instability 117, 119
instructions 25, 67, 122, 135, 171, 173–4, 184
intellectual intelligence 44, 172
intellectual understanding 85, 92, 171
intelligence 44, 167, 172, 175
  intellectual 44, 172
intentions 11–12, 40–4, 113, 116–17, 128, 159, 172
interest 43, 51, 58, 61, 124, 131, 175, 178
intimacy 104–5
  with all things 87–9
intoxication 123–4, 128
irritation 60, 76, 103, 133, 141, 146, 180, 182

jigsaw puzzle 171, 189
journeys 4, 16, 66, 85, 88, 90, 145, 148
judgements 132–3, 141, 146, 149, 157, 161, 197, 199
judging mind 122–3
juggling 49
jumping 12, 20, 159–60, 187

kaleidoscope 90, 102
karma 92–3
kāya 63
kindness, loving 2, 28, 101, 120
knots xiv, 106, 214
knowing 19–20, 35–6, 40–3, 96–7, 156–7, 190, 207–9, 213–14
  clearly 40–6, 55, 59, 85, 190
  the mind 77–8, 201
  objects 165, 201
  quality 43, 83, 97, 166, 190, 207, 209
knowledge, bare 24–5, 50

labelling 23, 64, 72–3, 136–7, 177–8, 185
  thoughts 149–53
language xiv, 88–9, 94–5, 98, 104, 144, 147, 167–8

lens 20, 64, 78, 93, 96, 101–2, 121, 124
letting go 59–60
life 5–7, 87–8, 114, 126, 146–8, 154, 203–4, 211
  daily 44, 72, 111
  spiritual 91, 125, 192–3, 206
lobha 123, 126, 131–2, 176 *see also* craving
long view 127–9
longing 122, 126, 128, 140, 214
loss 116, 133–4, 167, 213
love 2, 10, 12, 90, 116, 120, 146, 193
loving kindness 2, 28, 101, 120
Lubbock, Tom 167–8

Mahānāma 1
Matrix, The 192–3
meals 1, 67, 130, 183
meditation 3–4, 6–7, 11–13, 16–17, 41–3, 49–50, 52–5, 155–6
  formal 7, 44, 156
  practice 3, 7–8, 15, 34, 103, 110, 156, 170–1
  sitting 24, 43, 141
meditators 168
  bad 149
  good 149, 195
melodies 27, 203
memories xiii, 20, 35, 38–9, 62, 67–8, 77, 79–80
mental activity 62, 79, 108, 143, 150, 159
mental factors 17, 45, 62, 68, 121–2, 151, 207
mental faculties 143, 206
mental functions 78, 144
mental images 23, 62, 76, 128
mental objects 95, 101, 104, 124, 209
mental processes 61–2, 73, 78–9, 144
mental states 15, 101, 114, 122
mettā 28, 120
migraine 4, 137–8, 154
mind 2–22, 24–30, 49–63, 72–83, 95–112, 114–35, 155–91, 195–202
  attitudes of 28, 135, 211
  conceptualizing 20, 173
  identified with experience 163
  independent 138–40
  judging 122–3
  knowing 77–8, 201

stimuli 67, 70
stories 28, 30, 51–2, 146–51, 153, 158–9, 161, 165
storms 16, 79, 91, 188
storytelling mind 146–9
strong intentional thinking 158–9
subtlety 114, 196
suffering xiv, 3–4, 9–12, 15, 44–5, 53–4, 106–7, 175–6
  cycle of 113–41
sunlight 103, 170
sunshine 139, 186
surprise 35, 116, 125, 134

tactile sensations 62, 64, 66, 76, 145
tastes 62–3, 66–7, 73, 100, 122, 124, 199, 203
teachers 5, 16, 20, 100, 155, 165, 171, 182
Tejaniya, U 5–6, 25, 50, 74, 79, 92, 165, 171–2
temperature 21, 65, 117
tension 21, 30, 50, 54, 64–5, 110, 113, 199–200
  physical 51, 174, 210
thinking 20–2, 78–9, 143–8, 150, 152, 154–6, 158–61, 163–6
  about practice 182–3
  faculty 20, 143
  mind 20, 64, 149, 214
  power of 154–5
  process 147–8, 159
  strong intentional 158–9
thoughts 19–21, 64–6, 76–7, 79, 95–9, 101–5, 107–12, 197
  believing 156–8
  definition 159–60
  not the enemy 155–6
  labelling 149–53
  learning to see through identification with 160–2
  power 159
  proliferating 159
  types of 158–9
  wispy wandering 159
  working with 143–68
throat 21, 40, 67, 111
tickling, sensations 74, 94
tightness 21, 88, 123, 161–2, 184
tingling 47, 69

tone, feeling 8, 25, 62–3, 68–70, 72–5, 78, 81
touch sensations 63, 67, 124
traditions, Buddhist 15, 18, 92, 143, 170, 199, 225
training perspective 93, 105, 161
trees 2, 4, 14, 36, 103, 107, 115
trust 91, 100, 120, 127, 198
truth 29, 116, 157, 185, 192
TV 38, 66, 116, 127, 180

UK xiii, 33, 167, 225–6
unawareness 13, 153, 196–9
  focus on 196–8
  prioritizing 128
uncertainties 82, 154, 184
understanding 5, 85–6, 116–17, 155–6, 169–71, 174–6, 187–8, 206
  clear 4, 175
  intellectual 85, 92, 171
unfairness of life 114
unnecessary effort 50, 197, 209–10
unpleasant feelings 70, 75–6, 95
unpleasant objects 188, 195

Vajrapāṇi 199–200
values 5, 12, 41–2, 45, 146, 182, 206, 211
vedanā 68, 70, 73 see also feeling, tone
views 16, 20, 64–5, 73, 75–6, 91–3, 126, 184–6 see also Right View
  implicit 89–91
  long 127–9
  wrong 105–6
villages 38–9, 59, 118, 226
Vineyya Abhijjhadomanassa 52

wanting 100–101, 104, 119, 123–5, 130, 132–3, 137, 153
  mind 124–5, 128, 202
  not 119, 122, 130, 133–5, 156
warmth 19, 21, 42, 69–70
warp and weft 41–2
watching the mind 79–80
water 2, 33, 39, 103, 111, 118, 167, 203
weather 25, 114, 116, 133, 173, 186
wisdom 2–4, 6–8, 40–3, 85–8, 125–8, 165–6, 169–78, 187–9
  and awareness 6, 122–3, 162, 165, 173–4, 196, 198, 213–14

WINDHORSE PUBLICATIONS

Windhorse Publications is a Buddhist charitable company based in the UK. We place great emphasis on producing books of high quality that are accessible and relevant to those interested in Buddhism at whatever level. We are the main publisher of the works of Sangharakshita, the founder of the Triratna Buddhist Order and Community. Our books draw on the whole range of the Buddhist tradition, including translations of traditional texts, commentaries, books that make links with contemporary culture and ways of life, biographies of Buddhists, and works on meditation.

As a not-for-profit enterprise, we ensure that all surplus income is invested in new books and improved production methods, to better communicate Buddhism in the 21st century. We welcome donations to help us continue our work – to find out more, go to windhorsepublications.com.

The Windhorse is a mythical animal that flies over the earth carrying on its back three precious jewels, bringing these invaluable gifts to all humanity: the Buddha (the 'awakened one'), his teaching, and the community of all his followers.

Windhorse Publications
38 Newmarket Road
Cambridge
CB5 8DT
info@windhorsepublications.com

Consortium Book Sales & Distribution
210 American Drive
Jackson TN 38301
USA

Windhorse Books
PO Box 574
Newtown NSW 2042
Australia

THE TRIRATNA BUDDHIST COMMUNITY

Windhorse Publications is a part of the Triratna Buddhist Community, an international movement with centres in Europe, India, North and South America and Australasia. At these centres, members of the Triratna Buddhist Order offer classes in meditation and Buddhism. Activities of the Triratna Community also include retreat centres, residential spiritual communities, ethical Right Livelihood businesses, and the Karuna Trust, a UK fundraising charity that supports social welfare projects in the slums and villages of India.

Through these and other activities, Triratna is developing a unique approach to Buddhism, not simply as a philosophy and a set of techniques, but as a creatively directed way of life for all people living in the conditions of the modern world.

If you would like more information about Triratna please visit thebuddhistcentre.com or write to:

London Buddhist Centre
51 Roman Road
London E2 0HU
UK

Aryaloka
14 Heartwood Circle
Newmarket NH 03857
USA

Sydney Buddhist Centre
24 Enmore Road
Sydney NSW 2042
Australia

Introducing Mindfulness: Buddhist Background and Practical Exercises

Bhikkhu Anālayo

Buddhist meditator and scholar Bhikkhu Anālayo introduces the Buddhist background to mindfulness practice, from mindful eating to its formal cultivation as *satipaṭṭhāna* (the foundations of mindfulness). As well as providing an accessible guide, Anālayo gives a succinct historical survey of the development of mindfulness in Buddhism, and practical exercises on how to develop it.

A wise and helpful presentation of essential elements of the Buddha's teaching . . . it will be of great value for those who wish to put these teachings into practice. A wonderful Dharma gift. – Joseph Goldstein, author of *Mindfulness: A Practical Guide to Awakening*

A gold mine for anyone who is working in the broad field of mindfulness-based programs for addressing health and wellbeing in the face of suffering – in any or all of its guises. – Jon Kabat-Zinn, author of *Meditation Is Not What You Think: Mindfulness and Why It Is So Important*

Bhikkhu Anālayo offers simple skilled mindfulness practices for each of the dimensions of this book. Open-minded practices of embodied mindfulness are described, beginning with eating and health, and continuing with mindfulness examining mind and body, our relation to death, and the nature of the mind itself. Significantly, by highlighting the earliest teachings on internal and external mindfulness, Bhikkhu Anālayo shows how, individually and collectively, we can use mindfulness to bring a liberating understanding to ourselves and to the pressing problems of our global, social, modern world. We need this more than ever. – Jack Kornfield, from the Foreword

ISBN 978 1 911407 57 7

£13.99/$18.95/€16.95

176 pages

Satipaṭṭhāna Meditation: A Practice Guide

Bhikkhu Anālayo

Buddhist meditator and scholar Bhikkhu Anālayo presents this thorough-going guide to the early Buddhist teachings on *Satipaṭṭhāna*, the foundations of mindfulness, following on from his two best-selling books, *Satipaṭṭhāna* and *Perspectives on Satipaṭṭhāna*. With mindfulness being so widely taught, there is a need for a clear-sighted and experience-based guide.

Anālayo provides inspiration and guidance to all meditators, of any tradition and any level of experience. Each of the chapters concludes with suggestions to support meditative practice.

This is a pearl of a book. The wise and experienced teacher is offering Dhamma reflections, illuminating the practice of Satipaṭṭhāna *with a fertile and colourful lucidity. It is a treasure-house of practical teachings, rendered accessible with a clear and simple eloquence, and with praiseworthy skill and grace.* – Ajahn Amaro

This breathtaking Practice Guide *is brief, and profound! It offers a detailed, engaging, and flexible approach to* Satipaṭṭhāna *meditation that can be easily applied both in meditation and day to day activities.* – Shaila Catherine, author of *Focused and Fearless: A Meditator's Guide to States of Deep Joy, Calm, and Clarity*

Once more Bhikkhu Anālayo has written a masterpiece that holds within it an accessible and clear guide to developing and applying the teachings held within the Satipaṭṭhāna-sutta. – Christina Feldman, author of *The Boundless Heart*

Anālayo has developed a simple and straightforward map of practice instructions encompassing all four satipaṭṭhānas – *the body, feelings, mind and* dharmas – *that build upon one another in a coherent and comprehensive path leading to the final goal.* – Joseph Goldstein, co-founder of the Insight Meditation Society, from the Foreword

Bhikkhu Anālayo presents the Buddha's practical teaching of the path to nirvana in one comprehensive whole: the wheel of satipaṭṭhāna. *He writes for people who practise, and his own shines through like a beacon. This makes it a very exciting guide for practitioners – the truth of it leaps out at you.* – Kamalashila, author of *Buddhist Meditation: Tranquillity, Imagination and Insight*

ISBN 978 1 911407 10 2

£11.99 / $17.95 / €14.95

256 pages

Mindfulness of Breathing: A Practice Guide and Translations

Bhikkhu Anālayo

Buddhist scholar and teacher Bhikkhu Anālayo explores the practice of mindfulness of breathing in the sixteen steps of the *Ānāpānasati Sutta*. This is an authoritative, practice-oriented elucidation of a foundational Buddhist text, useful to meditators whatever their tradition or background.

In the first six chapters Anālayo presents practical instructions comparable to his *Satipaṭṭhāna Meditation: A Practice Guide*. The remaining chapters contain his translations of extracts from the early Chinese canon. With his accompanying commentary, these help the practitioner appreciate the early Buddhist perspective on the breath and the practice of mindfulness of breathing.

Anālayo presents his understanding of these early teachings, arising from his own meditation practice and teaching experience. His aim is to inspire all practitioners to use what he has found helpful to build their own practice and become self-reliant.

In this book Bhikkhu Anālayo explores the seminal topic of ānāpānasati *with characteristic thoroughness, openness and skilful reference to the textual tradition behind this practice. Through linking the central theme to topics such as walking meditation and the aggregates, he broadens its relevance to a wide range of Dhamma-cultivation. Here then is a valuable resource for us to dip into, or to steadily work through, to gain access to this liberating practice.* – Ajahn Sucitto

Bhikkhu Anālayo's genius is, in part, to analyse the terse, sometimes obscure language of the Buddha's discourses and reveal them as fresh, practical guidance for contemporary meditators. Here the author takes up the discourse on mindfulness of breathing to lead us phrase by phrase into clear, precise instructions to calm the mind and realize the Buddha's deepest insights. The most complete and in-depth guide available for this classic meditation. – Guy Armstrong, author of *Emptiness: A Practical Guide for Meditators*

Practical, inspiring, thought provoking! This book achieves two great aims. First it offers meditators a clear practice sequence that is easy to apply. And second, it presents new translations and thoughtful analysis based on a comparative study of early Buddhist texts. This practical and thoughtful interpretation of the Buddha's sixteen steps will surely inspire readers to re-discover the joyful and liberating potential of mindfulness with breathing. – Shaila Catherine, author of *Focused and Fearless: A Meditator's Guide to States of Deep Joy, Calm, and Clarity*

ISBN 978 1 911407 44 7

£14.99 / $19.95 / €16.95

320 pages

It's Not Out There: How to See Differently and Live an Extraordinary, Ordinary Life

Danapriya

Most of us constantly look outside ourselves for something: happiness, love, contentment. But this something is not out there. 'It' is within us. We are full of these qualities: happiness, love, contentment and more.

In *It's Not Out There*, Buddhist teacher and mentor, Danapriya, helps you to look inside yourself in such a way that life becomes more vivid, joyful and extraordinary.

If you want to suffer less and to live life more fully, this book is for you. It's about seeing the reality of the human predicament, and seeing through the illusions that create unnecessary pain for yourself and others. This book uncovers the fertile ground of your own potential, and enables you to live the life you are here for. Stop, look, listen and sense, you are worth it.

'Written in simple, down-to-earth language, It's Not Out There *is brimming with practical wisdom. Positive and encouraging, Danapriya shares ways to help anyone who wants to change their life and find greater happiness and fulfilment.'* – Dr Paramabandhu Groves, co-author of *Eight Step Recovery: Using the Buddha's Teachings to Overcome Addiction*

'Reading this book is like having a conversation with a wise friend – someone who doesn't just talk at you but who is interested in your thoughts and experience too. Buy one for everyone you know who is serious about life and how to live it well.' – Subhadramati, author of *Not About Being Good*

Born Ian Dixon in 1959, Danapriya ('one who loves giving') has been involved in personal growth and healing work for over three decades. Ordained into the Triratna Buddhist Order in 2001, he founded the Deal Buddhist Group in Kent, UK, in 2007. Based there, he continues to lead retreats and teach meditation, while also running the counselling business *Talking Listening Clarity*. www.danapriya.org

ISBN 978 1 911407 59 1

£9.99/$13.95/€11.95

160 pages